THE
BEAUTY
OF BEING
HUMAN

P O E M S

Nirander Safaya, Ph.D

ISBN 978-1-967362-22-6 (paperback)
ISBN 978-1-967362-23-3 (hardcover)
ISBN 978-1-967362-24-0 (digital)

Printed in the United States of America

In loving memory of my wife,
Shama Fotedar Safaya, B.Sc., M.Sc.

June 4, 1941 – March 17, 2020

In Praise of
Reflections on Being Human: Poems

BeautifulNow listed Nirander Safaya's *Reflections on Being Human* as one of the 10 most beautiful poetry books published in 2016, which included *The Collected Poems* of W. B. Yeats; and commented that "Safaya indulges in more romantic and spiritual aspirations, delving into universally perplexing existential questions about human nature and experience…Joy, sorrow, love, and loss are all poked and prodded in the search for true peace and happiness, as expressed by 152 beautiful poems."

—beautifulnow.is

"[These] poems have a rare intellectual and spiritual depth as well as lyricism. That they are written in a formal style makes them even more appealing."

—A. Spencer, Editor for iUniverse

"Nirander Safaya's extensive collection of poetry, *Reflections on Being human,* covers subjects from immediate to divine…Works toward truth and self-actualization with many poems hinting at ultimate, perfect unity… Strong narrative tendencies and surprising imagery make this collection a frequent surprise… A sensory delight…A dazzling reflective mix… to uncommon and timeless effect."

—Foreword Clarion Review

"This earnest collection tackles serious questions… Considers the subject of love both abstractly and concretely… Some pieces are joyful, full of appreciative gratitude… [Some] verses turn darker… [Some] become philosophical."

—Kirkus Review

"[Safaya] contemplates concepts and emotions as diverse as sorrow, acceptance, regret, hope, desperation, peace, chaos and order, pleasure and pain, responsibility, grace and karma."

—Blueink Review

Contents

Author's Note

This book, titled *The Beauty of Being Human,* contains two hundred poems written after my retirement from a scientific career. Most of these poems came out first in 2016, in a book titled *Reflections on Being Human,* published by iUniverse, USA. To the present volume, fifty new poems have been added, and some of the previously published ones have been slightly revised. Hence, *The Beauty of Being Human* is a revised and enlarged edition of *Reflections on Being Human.*

The motivation for presenting the entire collection to my readers remains essentially the same as was expressed in the preface of the previous edition (see next page). My quest, particularly, has been to express in verse my deepest appreciation of life and its marvelous gifts of love, light, and consciousness to the humankind (*Homo sapiens*).

We sapiens are highly evolved and blessed beings on this planet Earth—a tiny "blue dot" in the vastness of the universe. Besides being capable of meeting the basic requirement for survival, sapiens display a vast array of feelings, thoughts, and behaviors that range from the most ordinary to the most sublime. Issues like science versus religion, matter versus spirit, logic versus emotion; or questions about life, love, truth, beauty, joy, disappointment, death, afterlife, etc. have persistently appealed and intrigued us throughout the ages. My poems reflect on these aspects of human nature and its awesome beauty.

I see tremendous beauty and privilege in being a human because in spite of all the difficulties, defeats, challenges, and sorrows experienced in our lives, we keep on trying and progressing to a higher ground. This is, perhaps, due to the reason that our *consciousness* has an inherent desire and faculty for seeking love and knowledge for *its own* perfection. The perfection that is required to fully understand the *truth* behind all *appearances* and *existence* itself.

My poetry endeavors to capture a glimpse of what it means to be human and how we can see and transcend our shortcomings. This year the whole world has been gripped by the menacing pandemic of the coronavirus COVID-19. However, we are fighting this existential threat with incredible courage and hope. This too affirms the beauty of being human!

Nirander Safaya
Leander, Texas

Preface to the Edition
Reflections on Being Human

Many people think that science and religion are incompatible, and "never the twain shall meet." This feeling persists despite the fact that both these domains endeavor to find *truth*. Both place full faith in their own methods and findings, whether they are based on a mathematical equation, scientific experimentation, intuition, spiritual revelation, or hymns that touch the soul. In the same vein, poetry offers a unique medium to explore and express the truth and beauty of human nature and our aspirations for aesthetic and spiritual fulfillment.

Any attempt to bridge the gulf between the scientific and spiritual visions of humankind is useful. It leads us to discover and accept *truth* without compromising our faith in ourselves, our heritage, and the spirit and purpose that underlie our existence. Poets and philosophers have played a significant role in this process for centuries. Because of the inherent aesthetics and figurative power in poetry, its thought content is generally easier to digest than that of science or philosophy.

Having worked as a scientist for forty years, with an abiding interest in world literature, philosophy, and religions, I was tempted to paint some of the realities of life with the evocative brush of poetry. So after my retirement, I began to write poems about life, love, and light to illustrate how our ordinary experiences lead to self-knowledge and some understanding of human and divine nature. I chose poetry because of its precision, as science has, and its appeal to feelings, as religion has. Besides, poetry leans on philosophy for its ethics and aesthetics.

In this collection of my poems, *Reflections on Being Human*, I have tried to catch some glimpses of the joys and sorrows of life and love, and the saving grace of light—all of which contribute to human experience and existence. I hope my readers will take some comfort in thinking that hard facts and soft feelings can coexist and that our scientific and spiritual paths for discovering *truth* will eventually get closer. In the meantime we must continue enjoying life in all its multiple forms of art that deeply touch our heart.

Nirander M. Safaya
Austin, Texas
November 16, 2015
iUniverse revision date: February 3, 2016

Acknowledgments

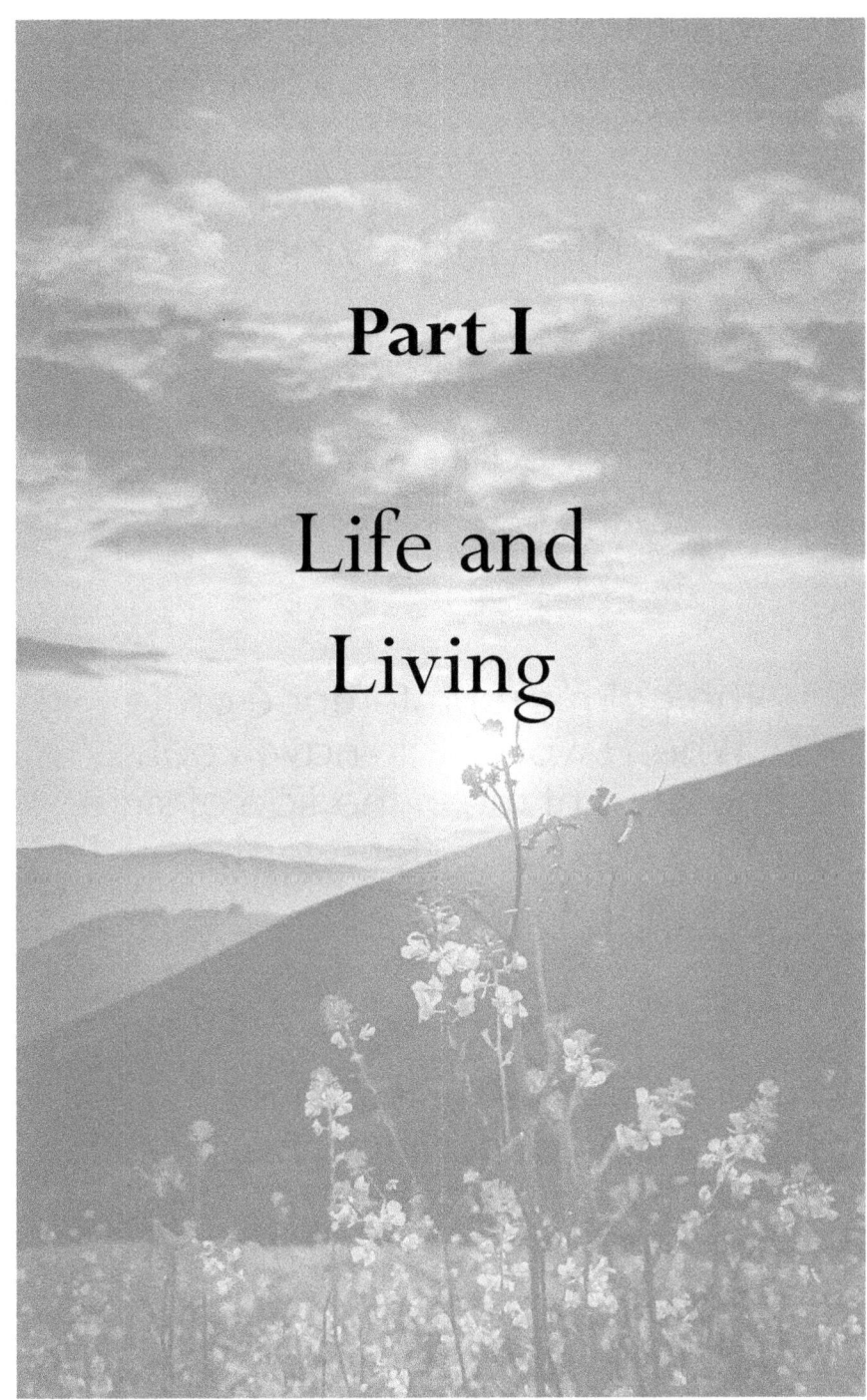

Part I

Life and Living

Life and Living

The unexamined life is not worth living.
—Socrates

The calm circumference of life
When I would fain have kept,
Time caught me in the tide of strife
And to center swept.
—Hafez

The universe is change;
Our life is what our thoughts make it.
—Marcus Aurelius

ඥ 1 ෬
An Aspiring Reed

---○---

This little flute of a reed thou
hast carried over hills and dales,
and hast breathed through it
melodies eternally new.
—Rabindranath Tagore, *Gitanjali*

---○---

I was just a dry, hollow reed
Till you punched seven holes in me!
Now you can put it to your lips
And hear my live melody.

Oh! if I were so lucky
As to inhale your divine breath
And turn it into seven notes of music,
I would surely conquer death.

My life has longed for sweetness:
Of thought, speech, and deeds;
But to master this music,
My soul your love needs.

The reed you picked to fashion
Into an ordinary flute
Came from a marshy little lake,
Where the lotus also grew—saluting you.

So if you find me unworthy
To grant me the boon I so desire,
Then rate me for the company I kept,
Standing in the same murky pool
With the lotus flowers—praising You.

ೞ 2 ೞ
My Life and Longings

— o —

What mortal, when he saw,
Life's voyage done, his heavenly Friend,
Could ever yet dare tell him fearlessly:
"I have kept uninfringed my nature's law"?
—Matthew Arnold, *Human Life*

— o —

Oh, I have yet to go a few miles more,
Make a few calls at this and that store,
And visit one more beckoning shore
Lest I forget to pay what I owed before.
Let me finish this business and nothing more.
Then I will see you.

In the budding spring of my youth,
I didn't look for the hidden truth,
For love and learning came naturally smooth.
All was arranged neatly in its assigned booth,
But without any sense of the missing truth.
Then did I think of you!

The glory of summer was no simple matter.
There were many desires to quench
And hungry passions to feed—sooner than later.
In these pursuits, there were some egos to flatter.
Right or wrong, success alone seemed to matter.
Then did I think of you!

As the summer peaked, new vanities grew,
Drawing attention to things I hardly knew;
For the glamour of power and position in society,
A fuzzy line between prowess and prudence I drew.

My passion for sham recognition demonically grew.
Then did I think of you!

Now, when I am old and in the season of fall,
The green in nature having turned gold,
A strong voice seems to persistently beckon and call,
Lifting its eye from books of yore, encompassing all
That matters most—dear God, I will not fail or fold.
Now I crave to see You.

℘ 3 ℘
The Journey

———————————— o ————————————

Childhood fancies make us grow,
Youth's urges keep us on the toe,
The prime of life tells us to sow
Seeds of trust—for love to grow.
Old age brings us a marvelous gift.
First, it does our many burdens lift:
We don't carry the same old ego,
For with time, we grow mellow.

Each child comes with God's gift,
Given as parental love and genes
That determine our base and tilt,
Our raw nature and adaptive skills.
Thus nature and nurture combined
May shape us into a person divine
Or make us a creature of evil mind,
And each of these gives its own sign.

From early on we begin to explore
The world around and within us,
Feeding on knowledge and more,
Generally without too much fuss.
But soon our focus shifts to love
(First to the earthly, then divine)
That touches us gently from above,
Guiding us by its power sublime.

At each stage of our trenchant life,
We encounter some joy and strife;
Neither remains too long with us,
But we can't our feelings suppress.

All pursuits arise from love or hate;
These in turn determine our fate.
Of all the drivers, love is the best,
For it keeps us flying over the crest.

❧ 4 ❧
The Enchanted Hill
———————— ◇ ————————

Step by step, arm in arm, we ascend the live hill.
Steep and rugged though it is, a passionate thrill
Keeps us going without rest, to test our restless will
And see the truth that lies behind the enchanted hill.

It is no ordinary hill of earth and rock and scrub,
Nor is it pointed skyward as a tall, tangible nub—
Challenging our muscles and sinews to grind or rub
Against its gritty side, without a shady tree or shrub.

The hill changes its shape with each step we take,
And after each moment—which is surely kept
Stored in memory—it morphs, as it deems apt,
Into something quite unknown and out of step.

Out of step, and unlike its past reality and repose,
It assumes a shape nowhere reminiscent or close
To its former semblance or purpose, as we suppose,
But a new state of being—an altogether new repose.

Call it as you may, but look deeply into its mystery:
The hill morphs to test our memory of its history,
Written by us and the hill together in live chemistry,
Recounting trials, toils, gains, and mind's mastery.

The enchanted hill feeds on our feelings and flesh;
It teases and tortures and then restores us afresh,
Kindling hope and purpose in our weakened breast
Until we scale its last hurdle in one leap of trust.

෴ 5 ෴
A Measure of Life

———————————— o ————————————

We fill and empty our minds each day,
Like coffee cups, soup bowls, and plates,
And wash our memories down the drain,
Just to make our lives simple and plain.

We rearrange the cupboards and closets,
Blow out the dust, wipe away the grime,
And rinse our hands to wash away time—
Its huge burdens and obligations prime.

We comb the stores and the countryside
In search of things we assume we need:
Food and drink for body and mind aside,
Casual lovers, passions, and desires to feed.

Like Sisyphus, tied to the rock of routine,
We fill the hours with our labor and love,
While our mortal frames westward lean,
Yet our efforts seem worthwhile somehow.

This routine appears right, and aptly so,
For there, indeed, all the pleasures do meet
Where love, labor and laughter together go,
And one's daily life is just, simple, and sweet.

❧ 6 ☙
Horizon

———————————— o ————————————

If only I could reach the horizon and stand
Where the earth rises to embrace the sky,
I could catch the heaven's azure in my eye
And touch the silvery clouds floating by,
While my feet are still on the solid ground.

The horizon is distantly circled around me,
But as I walk toward it from any direction,
It recedes away at the same pace,
Leaving me at its center, even if I race.
So I wonder what a challenge I face!

I have been walking toward the horizon
All my life—without any success in sight,
Calling worldly commerce my delight,
Beguiling time in its cycles of day and night.
Thus confined, my life will simply fade away.

I believe I should keep on going, searching
A way out of the conundrum of life's longings,
Cast away attachments, beliefs, and belongings,
And begin again earnestly to brace my will
For ending the agonies of my own making.

But if my efforts to reach the horizon fall shy,
Then let it come to me on its own wings.
I am ready to receive it on the hills or dales,
Seething deserts or rough seas lashed by gales.
For I want to touch the horizon before I die.

ଓ 7 හ
Signs of Life

—————————————— o ——————————————

From the lay of this piece of land,
Long abandoned, one can see
That generations of men and women
Lived and labored here—hand in hand.

The cottages with terraced gardens
That once stood proudly on this hill
Have all weathered and tumbled down
Time's slope without a frown.

A moving sense of form and beauty
In them who lived here is still visible
In the fallen arches and empty altars.
Dry fountains and sagging shelters.

But the air above the dirt and rubble
Is crisp and clear—like a new bell,
Still echoing with the songs and mirth
Poured here at each festival and birth.

The songs those men and women sang
Joyously with each other, and with life,
Must have been played in full tune
With the thrushes—welcoming June.

The sun and stars shine over this place
As before and seem to secretly know:
The life that was teeming here once
Hasn't been extinguished from thence.

A gentle breeze stirs the fallen leaves
On sunken roofs and the bare ground,
Like they want to come back to life;
For here, indeed, lust for life was rife.

I wonder: What happened to those
Who once vigorously thrived here!
Was it some grim disease or drought?
Or just Time's ever-streaming rout!

Time is a mysterious old gypsy man.
It bestows mercies and glories—as it can,
Depending on people's good will and skill,
Leaving then to nature its mission to fulfill.

ೞ 8 ೩
A Measure of Time

— 0 —

Motion of bodies in space
Becomes time,
As the moving hands of a clock
Or the beats of a pulsating heart,
Each jogging at its own pace,
None leaving a lasting trace.

Like an elastic string in a lace,
Time is a yarn in the fabric of space,
But without a recognizable face—
So much like mortal love,
Which comes into its being
Only when we are actually living.

We like to keep track of all events,
Even silly thoughts that come and go
Or the emotions that set us high or low.
But there is nothing that prevents
Time from its insensate flow
Through our fingers—fast or slow.

It is easier to invoke fate
Than to ask of time a favor:
To lead us away from the open gate
To perdition and God's disfavor.
For time has a cruel streak:
It turns us all old and weak.

So let us keep on moving,
At our own sweet pace going.
It isn't being early or late
That changes our fate,
But the labor of love
That gets rewarded somehow.

ଓ 9 ଈୠ

now

———————— o ————————

o my love,
where shall i start?
in the mind or in heart!
the one is empty and still,
the other filled to the brim.
sorrow found a cozy place
in my heart's free space
and drained my mind
of its will to face,
o dear God,
my loss,
alas!

as i go
racing down
the memory lane,
searching through the
cold, ashy ruins of my past,
i find there nothing worthy
to ponder about or possess—
just a few scraps of rusted
metal buried in the soul.
then it comes to me:
i too had, once,
some grit
in me.

now as
i consider duly
the path i must take,
which may lie betwixt

that one of my choosing
or of destiny's own doing,
i should remold the ashes
of my past into a dense
block of gritty steel
fired in the fair
mercy and
will of
God.

൸ 10 ൸
My Sheltering Abode
―――――――――― o ――――――――――

Hugging the contours of life
Along the steep mountain side,
Negotiating hair-pin bends
Hidden by the jetting rocks
(That stoically time abide!)
Casting morphing shadows
On the narrow winding road,
I drive to my sheltering abode.

I wish it were the sea shore
By which a wide curving road
Took me to my awaiting door:
Through the sun-drenched mist
Pierced by heady palm trees
Standing as phantoms of yore,
Holding out their silver keys,
Beckoning me to my fair lees.

Why do the treacherous roads
Suddenly appear in my way!
Infusing undue fear and caution,
Asking for too much precaution,
Thus taking away my freedom?
Yet fueling my raw excitement
And subsiding my boredom
With their shock treatment.

Is it because I am just a pawn
Controlled by an alien plan?
But whose plan could that be!
Not of God or of my destiny,

For I am in Him, He in me,
Together charting a course.
So why should I worry at all,
For don't I His promise recall?

The road that takes me home,
Though tortuous it may be,
Shows a way to say goodbye
To my self-imposed austerity
And the fear of driving all alone,
Knowing that God is watching,
And my Love is eagerly waiting
To hold me against her bosom—

Both of them my sheltering abode.

ೞ 11 ೞ
Here and Now

———————————— o ————————————

I see now, it is the Here and Now
That beckon me most; not as how
Ego's impetuous brother, Id, tugs
Hard to enjoy the Dionysian drugs,

But to make up for the time lost
In remembrances that dearly cost
And future dreams that don't last.
So to Here and Now I hold fast.

The past is done; it can't be undone,
Not a line, dash, or dot made in fun
By wit or magic unwrit or erased;—
This truth about Past must be faced.

Future flies in expanding space.
There infinite chances one shall face
In the changing reality of the world
Wherein all of us are helplessly hurled.

Verily, Here and Now is that point
Where Past and Future are conjoint:
Past is a shadow that exists no more;
Future a phantom never seen before.

The present has a real, tangible form;
Revel in this without doubt or alarm.
Rejoice in its life-affirming presence;
Dejection and death mark its absence.

I blissfully bow to the Here and Now.

෨ 12 ෪
Equus, My Equus
———————————— o ————————————

Equus! Equus! show me the way.
Don't hesitate, tremble, or sway,
For a noble path we must take;
Truth and beauty as one, we must make.
Our new destiny we must boldly face.
In this quest, doubt or fear has no place.

Equus, dear, you are strong and fair,
Of noble birth from a proud sire
And a beautiful mare, both full of fire.
So I don't see how we can tire
On this journey that we undertake,
For we have our destiny to make.

You remember my grand old man—
A dashing doctor of great repute
Who could help a mare bear her foal
And bring it out intact, body and soul!
Your ma and pa were mighty proud
When they saw you neighing aloud.

You were born a feisty chestnut brown,
With a white star on your noble crown.
You've white socks on all of your feet.
Your mane lashes the wind as you fleet.
I comb your long lustrous tail every day,
Brush your flanks as you nibble your hay.

You love apples and sugarcoated oats
And dream of jumping over the moats
To castles where captive maidens languish
And expect me to free them from anguish.
Equus, the old ways of conquest are gone.
Now we've to cross a different Rubicon.

You and I have traversed arduous roads,
But none as difficult as the one that bodes
Death of character through lack of courage
And loss of faith in the truth-in-beauty adage.
Equus, didn't I ask you to show me the way?
So give me strength to carry my cross, I say.

ଓଃ 13 ଜ
What I Fear

―――――――――― o ――――――――――

I dare not tell you
What I fear, earnestly,
For you may laugh at me;
But if it's sunny tomorrow,
I may feel differently.

I fear the wind may pick up
Tonight from the lee.
It will shake down
Many a flowering tree
For being closer to the sea.

It is the smell of salt and fish
That chokes the trees and me.
The wind is free and autocratic,
Gusting, lusting wildly
To denude a flowering tree.

ೞ 14 ಐ
Indifference
— ० —

There is a framed picture of my mom and dad
On my bedroom wall, facing east.
It catches the morning sun and the moonlight,
But not to my complete delight.

I don't look at the picture as often as I should,
Not because it is on my back,
But the light cast off the glass blinds my view
Of the persons in the picture true.

I have ignored too long to do what would be right:
Move the picture to a better site
So I might lay my eyes on the oft-forgotten faces,
Who beckon me to recall my traces—

Traces of the bygone childhood days happily spent
On or close to my mother's lap,
Gazing at her face, listening to her sweet lullaby,
With my father fussing nearby.

Also, of the days when school and games held sway,
And away from home I went
Their eyes following, filled with hope and pride,
Or anguished when defeated I cried.

Their gentle guidance throughout my early life—
The steady beacon that lighted
Each bend and curve of the life's highway I took
Moving forward, without a backward look!

My all too craving self assumed a robotic routine,
Held me captive to trite demands of life
And made me woefully forget my real aim:
To know myself, I must know whence I came.

৫ 15 ৯৩
Affliction

———————————— o ————————————

I opened my eyes after a blissful night,
But she had left, taking her bags along.
Only her perfume was lingering on
In the bedroom, where I didn't belong.

I thought she had gone to get some air
Or drink something to wake her up
And be ready to show again her flair
After she had emptied one more teacup.

But when she didn't show up by noon,
I began to wonder: What could it be
That tore her away from me so soon,
When she had all night clung to me?

A searing pain shot through my heart.
Weird phantoms sat on my chest
And kept pounding me a whole lot,
Asking questions I couldn't answer best.

When I was beat and at my wits' end,
The telephone rang and broke my spell.
It was she, telling me, "I had to attend
An early Mass for a guilt feeling to quell."

See, we had met only a month before
At a resort and sown mutual affection;
I was a drifter ready to come ashore,
But she was fighting a moral affliction.

ॐ 16 ॐ
Getting Old

———————— 0 ————————

I hate to grow old
Each day—day after day.
Time doesn't leave me alone;
It takes me away
Like a walking stick
In his swinging hands
That chops the air
But never evenly lands
On the solid ground
Where I want to stand
And watch the world's
Myriad colors together band
Into a shaft of pure light—
Colorless and transparent,
Welcoming and loving—
Making all things crystal clear.

If the currents and eddies
Of *Time* would leave us alone
We wouldn't grow old
Nor the same ideas clone
Day by day, year after year,
Of prejudice and cant
Ripping apart the world
At its most vulnerable seams
With proclamations and practices
Serving no purpose or goal.

O *Time*, I beseech you
To hold your fetid breath
And see the waste and death

That you spread in your haste
Dragging us along to a dead end
Where we can't straighten or bend.

I refuse to grow old
Under the yoke of *Time*
Listening to the same old music
On the radio and TV channels,
Tabloids and newspapers that spew
The left- or the right-leaning view
Without having a center or clue.
This is the loud noise of *Time*
Drowning our voice in slime.

If we can't break free
From the sharp claws of *Time*—
Its nuisances prime: sufferings,
Diseases, old age, and death—
Then God save us from its tyranny
By His proclaimed power and love;
Otherwise *Time's* rod and rule
Will keep prodding us to remain
In its cruel and fatuous company
Until we fade away into eternity.

ରେ 17 ഉ
Dear Partner

———————————— o ————————————

Fifty hot summers and fifty cold winters
You and I have smartly weathered together,
And between the two, in the spring and fall
Planted roses for attar[1] and colors to gather.

In our own small way, we made it through
The forest of life; even as the mists appeared
To block or let the sunlight come through,
We kept on driving forward quite undeterred.

Each of us brought our strengths to bear
On the demands of relationship and care,
Facing toughest challenges without fear,
And the daily labors that too wear and tear.

Our passions weren't of a particular kind:
Love of reading and gardening, we shared;
In cooking and cleaning, we always shined,
But in the choice of music a little differed.

Our love for each other had its own phases,
Like the monthly cycle of moon in the sky—
Waxing and waning, feigning to ignore
Our cravings, but never failing to gratify.

In the early and middle sections of our life,
We would chase each other with desire—
Deeply intense and persistent in its demand,
And every time each other's faculty admire.

———————————

1 Essence of roses

And we were duly blessed with children,
Whose achievements made us very proud,
For services they rendered to their country,
Which made them stand out in a big crowd.

Today, at seventy-four, you look the same pretty
Woman whom I have loved in my own silly way.
But I wouldn't dare call you my old flame,
For you'll quit speaking to me on your birthday—
Which is today! And I say, "Happy Birthday, my Love."

ल 18 ल
To My Children

———————————— o ————————————

There are joys—but none so great
As living your life in a peaceful state,
Without strife, sorrow, or merciless fate,
And drinking from life at a steady rate.

The aims of life shift as grains of sand.
They seem real until we truly understand
The color and contour of the very land,
The mountain or valley where we stand.

Our senses and soul must clearly behold
The merits in ideas on which we are sold,
The acts we commit that seem so bold;
Thus we see what is and isn't real gold.

None of this is totally unknown to you,
For you have stood in that awesome pew
Of the morphing world, where just a few
Become self-aware and are reborn anew.

ॐ 19 ॐ
Daughter

Ω

Like earth, the bringer of life and bounty,
Like air, the ensurer of breath and beauty,
Like water, the awakener of spirit and body,
Like fire, power supreme and purifier of all,
Daughter, you are the life-giving mother
Of mankind, blessed and kind,
A treasure to find.

In you, daughter, resides the strength
Of fire and the music of water in motion,
The healing touch of air present all around,
The blue glow of the earth seen from afar.
Daughter, you bring purpose to mankind,
Joy to man, solace to child,
Soothingly styled.

Your name has a deep meaning, Seema.
It was given to you by your doting mama,
Defining the expanding frontier or territory
Of an empire, or any thought's trajectory
Acquired by the sheer brilliance of mind
And endeavor of the right kind
That the wise find.

ॐ 20 ॐ
Gia

─────────────── o ───────────────

When I heard the first cry of life
Issue from your trembling lips,
Taking in the first divine breath,
I felt a tingling in my fingertips.

A chorus of joyous feelings arose
In symphony, like strings of light,
When we caught the awesome sight
Of a child, lovely as a perfect rose.

Suffused by your mother's love,
You came regally to rule and tame
Our hearts and minds in your name,
Gabrielle S. T., our cute little dove.

They groomed you at a petite sink;
The nurse's hands were full and pink.
Papa stood nearby to see and show.
You held his pinky and didn't let go.

Neatly swaddled, you went to see
Your dear mama and whispered
Quietly in her ear, "It is me, Gia.
Come to show the way forward."

Your mama kissed your crown
And, pulling you close to her heart,
Whispered, "Yes, love, why not?
Say, are your eyes blue or brown?"

Then you looked deep into her eyes
And whispered this: "Does it matter:
Hue, color, or love? I take the latter;
For that is the truth that never lies."

৫ 21 ৯
Ashley

———————————— o ————————————

O Ashley, sweet, bright, lovely child, light of my eye:
How deeply happy and blessed we are. Don't ask why;
As you grow, you will know how stars shine in the sky,
How little buds drink the rainbow and bloom by and by.

Oh Ashley, sweet, bright, lovely child, light of my eye:
You came in a storm; your will and strength made it shy.
It hovered briefly and then vanished with a wimpy cry.
You won fair and square; we thanked God, the Most High.

Oh Ashley, sweet, bright, lovely child, light of my eye:
As your mom-dad-bro were trying to know you better,
My Rose of Austin would roll her eyes in anger and cry,
"Where is Papa? It ain't fair; I want him here and nearby."

Oh Ashley, sweet, bright, lovely child, look into my eye:
For four weeks your papa turned and tossed. Ask why.
Just to hold my dear granddaughter, my little cutie pie,
Touch her dainty hands and feet, and sing her a lullaby:
"Sweet wonder and delight, oh precious light of my eye."

✆ 22 ✇
Out of Memory
———————————————— ○ ————————————————

We were sitting outside on our porch,
Sipping cold coffee—with averted eyes,
Fearing conversation may snap our ties
And the sharp sunlight may hit our eyes.

But I couldn't help asking the question:
"Did we ever have any joy in our lives?"
At this, she rose and silently sped away,
Leaving me there with a sense of dismay.

I turned my head toward the dry yard—
Baked hard by the sun, thirsting for rain.
The few plants standing still were in pain;
At this desolation, my hope was charred.

She walked back to the porch and said,
"How come you don't irrigate the lawn?"
I remained quiet, uncertainly withdrawn,
And led my tired legs toward the shed.

There I sank in a chair to take a break.
My long life flashed by me stage by stage;
The childhood, youth, prime, and old age
Had been spent in trying my life to make.

But now I couldn't my priorities rethink,
Or figure out easily which turn to take;
Too much was on my plate and at stake.
Whatever I did would raise another stink.

She knew our water supply had been cut
For not having paid our bills on time.
But she couldn't this ladder easily climb,
For she had her mind from all reality shut.

I had seen this symptom in some old-timers
But never thought her condition to be serious,
Until her spells became frequent and obvious.
Then my love was found to have Alzheimer's.

≪ 23 ≫
Silent Treatment

———————————— o ————————————

Don't mock me with your silence.
It harms me not, but only you.
Your consuming pride and ego
Are at work—hardly affecting me.

Silent treatments won't make me cry,
But they make you fall from my eye.
You have played this game before
Without eliciting from me any reply.

Your vanity has inflated your ego,
Covering you in its dark veil,
Making you walk like a shadow,
Silently screaming, "Hell," to no avail.

Beauty is a noble gift; wear it well.
Pleasant speech adds to its content,
For it is the expression that can tell
If you are a beauty or a malcontent.

Silence has many hues and meanings.
When used wisely, it is golden.
When used in rancor, it is rotten.
Reach inside to figure your feelings.

There is a centering light in all of us.
It is the source and seat of conscience,
Always there to provide us guidance.
Just look for it with some eagerness.

∞ 24 ∞
Sing My Pain Away
——————————— o ———————————

I sing to the earth when it grieves
I sing to the wind when it moans
I sing to the river when it groans
I sing to the rain when it falls
I sing to the snowflakes when they melt
I sing to the babies when they cry

> My songs calm their grief.
> My songs are also taken up
> By the birds of air and water
> To calm down the elements.

O my Love:

How many strands of my song have you
                    picked up from the ground!
How many shouts of sheer joy have you
                    caught in your throat to echo!
How many lamentations of mine have you
                    held to your aching heart!
And how many times has your spirit moved
                    you to sing along with me!

Yes, my Love, you have many a time…
And found it comforting you too—
Whenever you're out of your patience,
Distressing over things that bothered you.

So, my Love:

Now it's me who needs you
To sing away my pain too.

❧ 25 ❧
Free at Last

In the urn for ashes
Lies my soul
Unconsumed and whole
Ready to Fly

I was once in an earthy mold
A form all could see
But now I am a cool flame
On its way home

When I was enmeshed in flesh
Feeding it with my own blood
I felt trapped like a fish
Now I am free as a bird

Carrying memories and knowledge
Of a lifetime of experience
Gained in pleasure and in pain
Leaving on my soul no stain

Hopefully I will see my maker
Where He presently dwells
But as I was told by my mentor
That God is present everywhere
So I can meet Him anywhere

೧೮ 26 ೪೦
I Am the Dust You See

—————————— o ——————————

Alas! I am not by your side now
To soften the anguish in your eyes,
And kiss the worries off your brow,
When you your sorrow can't hide.

The death of a loved one cruelly belies
Our hopes and dreams of a joyful ride
Through the changing landscape of life;
Yet life, or even death, we can't deride.

Just look at this: I was with you in life,
But after my death your memories of me
Are still alive in you—stirring in you
A passion to keep going with dignity.

My dust is still blowing around you,
Settling on your floor and coverings,
Kissing your feet and fingers softly
To let you know that I still love you.

You may not feel my presence there
Because my body has turned into dust;
But I am present in each tiny mote of it,
As you know it from the holy scripture.

So, my darling, don't be sad or anguished
By my sudden departure from this world;
You may be thinking I am unreachable now,
But that is not absolutely true, my Love.

ॐ 27 ॐ
Death of an Angel

———————————— o ————————————

How many loved your moments of glad grace,
And loved your beauty with love false or true;
But one man loved the pilgrim soul in you,
And loved the sorrow of your changing face.
—W. B. Yeats

———————————— o ————————————

She was silently dying each day
In front of my anguished eyes!
My tough angel, my love, my lovely wife
Was caught in the creeping claws of cancer,
Suffering immense pain, uncertainty, and strife.
She braved the tortures of cancer and its therapy
With a smiling face, but to no avail.

So she remained—for months confined
In a bed—nursing her pain, but unresigned.
The light in the room would, at times, gasp
As the air faltered to fill her lungs with life.
Sometimes a breeze came looking for her
To cool with its wings her perspiring brow.
How her silky hair started disappearing now!
She made jokes about it, just testing my love.

The white walls of the room stared sadly
At the occupied bed and the glass shelves
Groaning under the weight of pain, pain-pills
And medicines of all kind, but not really so kind.
My eyes were raining cold stones of sorrow;
I wondered if my sun would rise tomorrow!

Her pain would not leave her alone, nor I,
For I was there to catch her each and every sigh,
Holding back my own—not to make her cry;
As she was more concerned about my heart,
Which she thought may stop at any time.
But, obviously, God wanted *her* more than me.

See, both of us were dying in our own ways:
She was preparing to join the heavenly stars;
I was sinking deeper in this world's hell hole.
My Love left us all behind on March Seventeen,
In the year of coronavirus, beating COVID-19.
Now, in my Sorrow, I'm praying to see her soul.

෬ 28 ෩

Lament

─────── ○ ───────

O stagnant hours of night!
You keep me awake and suspended
By the long claws of your might,
Ripping me to no end in sight.

What pleasure, what satisfaction
Do you draw
In keeping me in your tight clutches,
Working on my nerves with a buzz saw,
As if I have broken some divine law?

Have I ever harmed you or any one!
Or forgotten to light my evening lamp!
Or placed myself above the sun!
Or prayed for time to come undone!

So why you keep me in suspended animation
Throughout the crawling hours of night!
Robbing me of my desire for consummation
And of my need for pious devotion—

In memory of my dear departed Love,
Who died because of the cold and damp
That had crept into my heart's camp
Without a tinder to fire up my life.

She was an admirable woman,
Only a few would compare to her:
In dedication, aesthetics, and charm;
But my cold indifference did her harm.

❦ 29 ❧
To Sorrow

————— ◦ —————

Why, O sorrow, do you sit in the kernel of my mind,
eating it away,
Layer by layer, like a treacherous worm, too unkind
in your sway?

Just for your own survival and indifferent to mine,
much too close
For comfort, pretending to be a friend—laying supine,
mocking in repose.

You of myriad forms and deceits are, at best, cold,
cunning, and meek.
You seek a warm, sheltering place in hearts bold,
then make them weak.

Shallow and shameless, you relentlessly prey
on sensitive souls;
Hunt and hound them until their hair turns gray
with your scolds.

Haven't I carried you tenderly as a mother would
her ailing child,
Sheltered you in my heart's ache as long as I could,
running wild?

O sorrow, don't you know why your obligation lies
with me?
I have given you a place in my heart that cries:
I am your home and you have the key.

෧ 30 ෨
Night
———————— 0 ————————

O Night—starry-eyed looking,
Reaching every heart and hollow
On the earth, you're searching
For the god of Love
Absent from the court of Jove.

The few hours you last
In a diurnal cycle, you press on
With your mission to surprise
The lovers in their embrace
And the sinners in their disgrace.

You will surely find him
Among flowers of all kind
Sleeping under your shadow,
Or comforting someone—forlorn,
Shedding tears alone.

O Night—how many secrets
Of humankind you want to know!
Yet we know how well you hide
And cover with your black blanket
All our sins committed day and night.

❦ 31 ❧
Mooning

─────────── o ───────────

When I raise my weary eyes
To see the moon in the skies,
She quickens her pace…
If the clouds block her face.

Wanting to draw attention,
She appears and disappears,
Changing her form and location,
Marking a calendar in space.

It's like the girl I once knew;
She wanted to be in full view,
No matter what she had on—
Often naked—dusk to dawn.

If time and space were infinite,
Then finite bodies could extend
Eternally, and so remain in it
Suspended, like the girl I knew.

ᏣᎦ 32 ᏍᎣ

Queen Moon

——————————— o ———————————

The stars around the lovely moon
Fade back and vanish very soon,
When, round and full, her silver face
Swims into sight, and lights all space.
—Sappho

——————————— o ———————————

The new moon is cradling the old in her arching arms,
Lending her an ebony glow from her crescent charms.
The young and old are in tight embrace as yin and yang.
The stars in the sky are still pouring out of the big bang.

I suppose numerous moons dance in our solar galaxy,
Each circling eagerly its own parent planet in ecstasy.
But is there anyone comparable to our Queen Moon,
Whose stately climb in the starry sky makes us swoon?

On clear nights, your cool radiance bathes us completely.
Night by night you grow your arc to a full circle, amazingly
Soothing our hearts' longings with your cool silvery light.
O Queen Moon, you rule us benignly to our sheer delight.

When you glide over the clouds that love to kiss your feet,
You treat us to a game of hide 'n' seek as the clouds meet
And disperse to veil or unveil your face, letting your light
Lend a silver lining, turning darkness into a hopeful night.

Man and beast and trees and mighty seas are in your hold.
You make man and wild beasts sing to you in ways untold.
You let *Raath-ki-Rani*[1] lend its fragrance to the new bride.
You command oceans and seas to swell and roll in pride.

It is said you were once a part of earth's mantle and core,
Then a demon carried you away, which left the earth sore.
Whatever the truth, we're still intimate and love you more;
That is why we keep on sending our ships to your shore.

---

1   A sweet-scented flowering tree

℃ℜ 33 ℘

Aegean Experience

---o---

Sitting around a big fire,
With blazing logs in a pit
Dug on the Aegean beach,
We serenaded the dolphins
Showing off in the sea.

The night was pearly gray.
The orange fireflies from the pit
Danced through the soft moist air,
Steaming off the backs of frolicking
Dolphins and the tangled seaweed.

Suddenly, Ulysses came to mind,
With his brave buddies
Recounting their odyssey.
We too fell in rhyme, remembering
Our pursuit of sirens and victories.

Each of us a yarn stretched,
Boasting of some daring feat.
Then someone laughed and said,
"Nothing has changed except costume!
Troy and Helen are still under siege."

CR 34 SO
Morning Beauty
——————————————— o ———————————————

The morning is slowly lifting her veil,
Revealing the beauty of hill and dale
Like a lovely bride opening her eyes
After a night of blissful sleep and sighs.

The morning air whispers in the glade,
Caressing each branch, leaf, and blade
Like a lass combing her silken tresses
Before she tries on her pretty dresses.

The dewdrops adorn blades of grass,
Quietly reflecting the color of brass,
Like tears of joy shining on the face
Of a ravished woman in purple lace.

An amber glow of soft light has spread
Over the valley and lit its church spires,
Like a smile on the face of a well-bred
Dame of firm faith that never expires.

The morning sun has raised its full orb
Over the valley dressed in emerald garb,
Like a celestial maiden lifting her head
Of golden locks from her heavenly bed.

The groves of trees and the rich verdure
Are inhaling the light to grow and mature
And flower like a budding young woman,
Consuming love to make another human.

The streams of the valley are awashed
In gold, melting the sunrays unabashed,
Like dancing beauties fluidly revealing
Their sinuous bodies to ignite a feeling.

The morning has stirred life in the valley.
Its domains and denizens prepare to dally,
Hugging cups of sweet tea or black coffee,
Starting their projects—whatever they be:

A parent is readying a child to go to school.
Some folks are keenly planning ways to pool
Their energy and resources for good use,
Like a resolute lady ready to ignite a fuse.

The men and women and children—all
Love their valley for it is like a cute doll
That gives them a great deal of real pride,
Like a young woman bedecked as a bride.

This blessed valley of exquisite mornings
Is a piece of paradise where no warnings
Or whistles are sounded under the sun
When a lovely lady plays nakedly in fun.

☙ 35 ❧
A Walk in the Woods

— o —

Come, let us venture into these woods—
Of sweet-scented pine and mottled shade.
Let's not keep looking for man-made goods
But enjoy Nature's bounty in front of us laid.
Look! the birds are flitting from tree to tree
Like the winged arrows of a rainbow we see;
Hear their melody sung from an inner decree
That lifts our hearts in bliss and sets us free.
Hear the music of the wind and rustling leaves
Under the shimmering eves of the happy trees.
See the undergrowth—lush green and tender
Touching our legs timorously in wonder.
Watch that bubbling brook vending its way—
Nourishing the verdure and washing away
Sand and clay as it merrily down the hill goes
Kissing shiny stones, mossy patches and tree toes.
A stiff breeze has lifted the tail feathers of a hawk—
Its eyes and ears alerted by a sudden squawk
From a small unsuspecting creature nearby—
Both of them looking for their food to survive by.
Observe closely that red line of ants marching
Resolutely up the drying limb of that pine tree;
They will laboriously gnaw and saw it to debris.
You don't get to see this breath-taking beauty
When you're indoors doing your humdrum duty.

ೞ 36 ೞ
Sun and Rain

Dance of light,
Music of rain,
Nourish our life
Over and over again,
Alike in pleasure and in pain.

The rhythms
Of birth and death
That come and go
Too fast or too slow
Carry us on in a single breath.

When the sun shines,
Hearts feel warm and gay;
Sparked by the golden eye
In the bright blue sky,
We say, "What a beautiful day!"

When it rains,
We're softly wrapped
In the rich aroma of the earth,
Dripping verdure and mirth,
And by this sweet symphony enrapt.

ཙ 37 ཪ
Spring Eternal

———————————— ० ————————————

The sun is slowly rising
Out of a vast live basin,
Shimmering liquid gold.

My heart is just emerging
Out of a deep, icy gloom
Into your blissful fold.

The light is now warming
The weary, cold east face
Of the mountain so old.

The spring is finally here,
With its color and music,
And I am no longer cold.

O spring! joyously fresh
Sun and rain, you bring,
Rekindling hopes untold.

Now, I am also awaiting
The spring of my youth
To make me feel as bold!

ॐ 38 ॐ
Promised Summer

---------- o ----------

O sweet little bird, I hear
You sing of coming summer,
When the spring is still here
In winter's whimsical care.

Far in the north, do we dare
Assume that seasons are fair
And their cycles quite clear!
But for your presence, dear!

So proclaim loudly, my fair
Angel of hope, without fear,
And bring the promised air.
I too shall lay my heart bare

And sing with you with flair,
For those who feel and hear
The coming of summer near
On the wings of hope, dear.

൙ 39 ൞
Heather's Hat

O Heather, O sweet Heather,
Your jaunty hat needs a feather;
Tomorrow, we'll go together,
A pheasant's feather to gather.

In the deep woods we will go,
Where fragrant flowers grow,
Where sparkling rivulets flow,
Like fireflies in the night glow.

In this place, the summer heat
Is cooled by a breath so sweet,
From a bed of heather so neat,
It makes hearts together beat.

There, in the perfumed glen,
The painted pheasants roam,
Strutting under an airy dome,
Dappled with gold, as in Rome,
Proud birds of nature's tome!

Pheasants can be quite onerous.
I will beg them to be generous,
To give a tail feather beauteous
For my lady's hat, to honor us.

ॐ 40 ॐ
Swallows

———————————— o ————————————

Five generations of barn swallows
Have claimed residency of a nest
Their two sleek ancestors chose
To build in my porch, facing west.

I saw the original pair first appear
In late March, surveying my place,
Checking the porch with extra care;
Then, eyeing a spot, they quickly built
A nest there, shaped like a low vase,
Nestled in a corner—with a jaunty tilt.

The nest's outer side was deftly girt
With small lumps of hardened dirt;
Its inside was feathered for comfort
And to protect their unborn from hurt.
I rarely saw these nesting swallows
During the day, but only once in a while,
When they darted swift as shadows,
Pursuing each other in a unique style.

The pair spent the nights together,
With their wings around each other,
The male sitting closer to the edge,
Making to his mate an avian pledge:
To raise a family from speckled eggs,
Feed them with insects caught in midair,
To strengthen their tiny wings and legs
And see them flying free here and there.

The mama bird would nod her head
Then bury her beak in his warm chest.
This game kept on going until it led
The mama to lay three eggs in the nest.

Soon the eggs hatched into tiny chicks,
Whose pale gullets I could easily see
As their yellow beaks did funny tricks
Whenever fed by their parents dotingly.

The awkward, scrawny, bald chicks
Were soon decked with slick feathers,
Alike in their parents' hues and optics.
Now, since the nest had no tethers,
They ventured out to test their wings
And see the awesome world around—
The thrills and challenges of all things
Up in the air and down on the ground.

My lovely guests left me in late May,
All the five of them, to my dismay.
I didn't realize that I had liked them so,
That their absence would make me low.
The nest was empty, as was my heart,
But little by little, it ceased to smart.
Then, the following year, a new pair
Of swallows I saw in my porch reappear!

They were like the ones I had seen before.
And as soon as they noticed the nest
(I couldn't their excited chirpings ignore),
They hugged it with their wings and chest.
Thereon, the new pair took its occupancy
Without any argument or further ado,
Respecting, I suppose, their urgency
Of the genetic dictate running through.

They repeated the same song and dance
As their parents had me learn before.
They too were blessed by life's chance
To raise a brood of their own to adore,
Without any visible bondage or remorse,
And then set them free on their course.

This drama played for three years more,
As three more generations of swallows
Came looking for their place of amore.
No wonder it is whence all life flows.

ೞ 41 ಐ
Bulbul[1]

———————————————— o ————————————————

A bulbul was hiding in a lush green bush
(Unaware of her ruffled toosh[2]),
Turning a merry song into a proper trill
For her lover with a gorgeous frill.

The bulbul's lover was in another bush.
He saw his sweetheart's raised toosh.
His heart beat faster, his legs made a push
To her swaying perch with a swishshsh…

Seeing her lover so close and near,
"Oh dear!" she cried, "I am glad you are here.
Hold me to your breast, my dear,
Let us make a love dance without fear."

They kissed and cooed on the beams of sun.
They puffed their feathers in sheer fun,
Then trilled and thrilled the bushes in unison;
When happily done, they flew as one.

---

1 A Persian songbird (*Luscinia golzii*)
2 A short gown (here, of feathers)

ⳤ 42 ⳥
Le Mina Bird

———————————— o ————————————

Pretty, sweet le Mina bird,
Your melody was heard
By the king and the clown,
In the forest and the town,
Where you sang the song
Of lasting love all day long.

Far away you may soon fly,
But the echo of your song
Will remain and never die
Or disappear from my eye.
It will bring great joy to all
In spring, summer, and fall.

Though immortal you are not,
But surely in your soft melody
Is a heavenly spirit so wrought.
It fills my heart in pure ecstasy,
Lifting my hopes beyond the sky,
As if the heaven were just nigh.

ᑫ 43 ᑭ
Kindred Spirits

————————————— o —————————————

"I don't know," she asked him gravely,
"Why those birds are flying so low?
There must be a cornfield nearby,
Where the grain has shattered off
The ripened cobs, otherwise, why?"

The wind last night was mighty high;
It rattled doors and broke a window.
And she had heard a bird's high-pitched cry.

She said, "I saw shards of glass scattered
Across the room, but none in the crib,
Where our babe slept quietly all night.

"When I went up to see him this morn,
He was fast asleep—apple of my eye;
His hair was windblown and straw dry."

Then, with eyes averted, she quickly added,
"As I kissed his head, he let out a shrill cry—
Like them birds, he seemed ready to fly!"

Amazed, he asked her in a hushed voice,
"Is our little one, then, one of them?"
"No," she said, "but then I don't know
Why some believe in being born twice!"

He cried, "Oh no, not that gibberish again.
I know some folks call it reincarnation!"
But he didn't know or cared to know:

The birds, with their swift wing and eye
Can see, smell, and dive from quite high.
They seek their food and rest and kin
Whenever and wherever they can find.
Their spirit isn't found in only one kind.

After a thoughtful pause, she ventured again,
"Some say consciousness connects us to all
But Avidya[1] and Maya[2] muffle its call
And, thus, our view of life remains small."

He was puzzled by her newfound views.

---

1   Lack of knowledge, or false knowledge
2   Power by which the material world is manifested but its reality hidden behind a veil.

os 44 so
Snow Geese

——————————— o ———————————

The framed shadows on my wall,
Colored in the gray demon's gall,
Raise their grim voices in a chorus,
Shouting, "Hang it, don't blame us."

I guess I am formed of dense clay;
Most things around me seem gray.
Thinking in circles devours my day;
In the valley of dark shadows I lay.

Should I stay or go away? Or think!
If I stay, I won't see that ray of light.
If I go, should I discard my baggage?
In this lies my blurred image.

Or stand on the granite seashore
And implore the mighty tides to restore
The broken wings of my thought,
So I may fly to wherever I ought:

Over the fields of ripening grain,
Over the emerald islands
About to rise again
And float there in the crisp blue air.

Or should I ask the silver moon
To relieve me of my baggage
And cast it on the tides of oblivion,
Where I can't gather it anymore.

Now, if the sea and moon see it fit
To grant me this boon,
I will become light and feel restored
To fly with the snow geese—soon.

༺ 45 ༻
Elements

---- o ----

The snow on the deck has melted and gone.
Green grass is trying to emerge in the lawn,
Pressing its pale, tender tips against the cold,
Crusty ice pinning it with unyielding hold.

Now, let us see, whose effort wins the race,
White Goliath or David Green, as they face
Each other in a deadly mortal embrace,
Their destiny determined by nature's pace?

The tepid sun, as yet in its early March run,
Is not sure how to help the grass and be done,
For it is also wrestling to break the crusty ice
And in this struggle keeps on rolling the dice.

My love, none can avoid the struggles of life.
They give us wisdom through pain and strife.
David Green, the grass, is meek and humble,
But in its great struggle, it does not tremble.

I have no doubt the sun will soon take away
The icy blues that have spread in the usual way
On each face and feature across the landscape
And restore our fallen spirits without escape.

ೞ 46 ೞ
All-Natural

──────────── o ────────────

A violent burst of rain
Hit the parched plain,
Leveling the anthills,
Nailing the window sills.
The small wild creatures
Hid in the sheltering features
Left on the bruised land,
With exposed veins of sand.

The ground cover on the plain
Was in minutes brutally slain.
The standing shrubs and trees
Were shorn of their leaves,
Denuded—they felt ashamed,
As if they had been gamed.
The birds had left the trees
To hide under a barn's eaves.

Ropes of water kept on falling
From the grim sky appalling.
There seemed no end in sight
Of the gloomy plain's plight.
Now, the inundated plain
Flowed in rivulets of pain,
Tearing away the black dirt;
Oh! the land's heart was hurt.

Deeply cut and badly eroded,
The soul of the soil was corroded.
With the roots now half-exposed,
The ground cover was deposed.

The eroded soil flowed down,
Turning the runoff dirty brown.
Through the thick curtain of rain
One could dimly see on the plain:

Two farmhouses close together,
With balconies facing each other,
And a large barn painted red—
Standing above a huge flower bed.
The cows in the barn were restless,
As if imbued with consciousness
Of the rainy season's ruthlessness.
But the rain god wasn't merciless:

He thought He was being very good
By ensuring bumper crop and food.
But the clouds weren't too happy
Because they were wet and wimpy.
Soon the sky appeared to clear a bit,
Allowing a soft band of light to hit
The two balconies facing each other.
Now, one could see without a bother:

A youth on each balcony there—
A boy and a girl watching a deer
Timorously crossing the plain,
Seemingly mindful of the rain.
The boy and the girl were clapping
Their hands, waving and flapping;
They were clearly admiring
The deer's pluck and daring.

The rainstorm's awesome force
Had changed their day's course,
Bringing them together once again
To watch the spectacle of rain,

As they had done on their third date,
While returning home too late
From a movie theater, where they
Had kissed, and a promise made.

❦ 47 ❧
Winter Fairy

———————————— o ————————————

Scene I

When the cold north wind blows
Over the Dakota Territory,
The life on the prairie
Rises to greet the Winter Fairy.
For her arrival, it's best to remember,
She may show up as early as September.
That is why the powwows and Octoberfest
Are held around this time with native zest.

When her herald spins on his gusty nave,
The grasses roll in a shimmering wave.
The leaves hanging still on the trees
Shake and rustle in musical keys
Before they fall to their knees
On earth's bosom to sleep.
Now is the time to apply caulk
On doors and windows to cold air block.

Scene II

Then on a gray November day,
The fairy sends us another herald,
A whirling flurry in a fleeting storm
Knocking softly on the window panes,
Showing us her smiling face—to inform
That the Winter Fairy is now on her way,
Planning for the next six months to stay
With us, making the prairie crystal gay.

As the Winter Fairy covers the prairie
In December, January, or February
With a thick mantle of dry snow,
The temperature falls low
Reaching zero
And below
Zero
And
Then
The blizzards blow.

Scene III

The Winter Fairy's noisy heralds cause no fear.
People go in and out of their homes
Bundled up in layers of looms,
Warm wool, and footwear,
Topped with insulated coats 'n' caps,
While the merry flurry dances and taps,
Whitening the roofs and less traversed lanes
Of the highways that disappear on the planes.
The powdery flakes that fall freely from the sky
Cover every exposed surface that meets the eye.

The soft snow then hardens into ice—just in trice
Trees and electric wires sparkle with hanging ice.
When the holy month of December draws near,
The Dakotans like to throw parties with fanfare.
They throng the indoor malls and warm shops
To buy gifts for the families—until time stops
The search—only to resume it the next day,
If the weather cooperates the same way.
For who knows what the Winter Fairy may bring
During the night as she and her heralds dance in a ring.

ശ 48 ജ
Windstorm

———————— o ————————

There is nothing which is not the subject
of debate, and in which men of learning
are not of contrary opinions.
—David Hume, *A Treatise of Human Nature*

———————— o ————————

The fierce wind that blew yesterday,
Breaking trees and shattering leaves,
Flattening ripening corn in the fields,
Raising dark clouds of dust and debris,
Sweeping clean the last paved street
In the village ravaged by savage heat
Left us wondering—what could it be!

Each group translated it differently
In their own language—effectively!

The believers said it was God's wrath
Lashing us for the sins we've committed.
The scientists blamed the CO_2 emitted
By our every fossil fuel–burning activity.
Some were opposed to the latter view,
Saying climate has a cyclical proclivity,
So humans must in no way feel guilty.

I was confused by these familiar views,
So I looked for other telltale clues.

The wind had blown away my senses,
Cooled down my blood and passion,
Dried up the puddles of my pure reason,
Released me from my raw emotion.

I found myself in a different season,
Washed and wiped clean, and cheery.

Then I realized the wind had no aim,
But to lift us from being too weary
Of the monotony of a torrid season.

ᘓ 49 ᘔ
Ganga Mata[1]

———————— o ————————

Out sprang from the head of Shiva[2]
(In deep samadhi on Mount Shivlinga[3])
A gushing stream of sacred waters
Meant to sustain the race of Arya.[4]

Down the mountain and the forests,
Wending its way through the plains,
The mighty Ganga[5] flows rapidly—
Unmindful of its banks and the bed—
Eroding them bit by bit silently
Hasting to meet her lover, the Sea.

O Sea! Tell your beloved to flow slowly
And see the flowering trees waving
From the falling banks gracefully—
Though endangered, standing bravely.

The rocks are showing their scars
With pride, slowly turning to sand;
The twinkling eyes of the stars
Fall on waters but don't see the land.

Krishna used to roam these banks
Searching for his beloved Radha.
In those days the banks stood firm,
As did the lotus breasts of Radha.

---

1 Mother Ganges
2 The third god of Hindu trinity
3 Name of a mountain range / peak
4 The Aryan tribes of north India
5 River Ganges

Time erodes the banks of memory
Where the gods once reigned proudly,
Protecting us and the Mother Earth,
But they too were caught in entropy.

❧ 50 ☙
Gathering Storm

In the eye of the storm
Lie no sounds of alarm;
It is in the turbulence around
Where signs of disaster abound,
That we must quickly sense
And prevent from doing harm.

When my Love looks at me softly
With a melting gaze in her eyes,
I know I am supposed to be
Attentive to her tapestry of lies.
And if I don't believe her, she cries.

Like a glass filled with dry ice
Collects dew on its outside,
Making it slippery as a dice,
Uncertainty kicks certainty aside,
Often making it tricky how to decide.

When my Love feels forlorn,
Neglected as an old, knotted tie,
I know she wants to be left alone
To practice taking sigh after sigh,
Which makes me close my eye.

When I see her walking quietly
Like a cat on its padded paws, to catch
An unsuspecting rat, I pick up quickly
My umbrella to escape the gathering storm.

❦ 51 ❧
On Freedom

——————————— ○ ———————————

O freedom! you know well your noble reach,
The extent of your domain over human speech,
The limits placed on daily action and expression
That cleverly bind you with undue suppression.

You are the firmament on which men and nations
Build their hopes for a just and prosperous world,
Seeking in you the protection of their passions:
Knowledge, action, beauty, and justice—unfurled.

You make an ordinary pen mightier than a sword.
You banish oppression and lift humanity upward.
You cast out prejudice of religion, gender, and race.
You are the formidable force we lovingly embrace.

Yet you face menacing challenges from all sides:
Warring nations, disputing factions, and the like
Invoke your name in vain, taking delirious rides
In the deserts of self-serving logic used as a dike.

There are the fanatic Freedom Fighters who prefer
To kill their own female kin—for exposing their face
Or for claiming their right to education—so suffering
In silence the malpractices of their religion and race.

Then there are those who want cleverly to legislate
New laws of religious freedom that could be used
As a tool against same-sex marriage and annihilate
The freedom of sexual expression—rightfully fused.

O freedom, some praise you for governance alone,
And some seek you for free-market system's hunger,
Yet there are many other powers you could us loan,
Such as freedom from ignorance, pride, and anger.

ca 52 so
Thanksgiving
———————————————— o ————————————————

We offer our thanks once a year—
That being the Thanksgiving Day!
The rest of the days we just stare,
Not even wondering what to say.

On this day we come prepared:
Alive, grinning, and very hungry
For the Thanksgiving Day bird—
Still roasting, not getting angry.

We honor this day by devouring
Basted turkey with family mixing
And the pilgrim ghosts hovering
Over the traditional dishes fixing.

It is a day when the adult children
Come for dinner, now once a year,
To see their old folks in confusion,
Still serving them who hardly care.

We first untie the legs of the bird,
Then pull its plucked wings apart
To expose the juicy breast, by most
Preferred, and serve it with fine art.

Some like the drumsticks or thighs,
But all go for the cranberry sauce
And other fixings with little cries
Of joy, as their hands reach across.

When the day's hectic delight is over,
We may silently thank our stars
For keeping the tradition surely alive,
And for the guests leaving in their cars.

C𝕽 53 ℬ𝕺
American Dream Life
——————————— ○ ———————————

We prefer order over chaos and believe
There's some meaning and purpose to life,
Which must be met one way or another;
So we get up in the morning, go to work
Or school, or laze around like the retired,
Who don't have to be on a set schedule.

The kitchen is the place where we love to feast
And imbibe, keeping nourished and going,
Chewing domestic issues and fresh news
Of our friends and neighbors—the world,
The warring factions in Washington, DC,
The bloody old disputes in the Middle East.

Then we pass our time shooting the breeze
With friends in our living rooms—to please
Our estranged spouses, suspended in time—
Taking our minds off the domestic discords.
Or we sportingly push our pouty girlfriends
To admire new faces, fashions, and trends.

Then there are the bedrooms we sleep in,
Alone or with another, perhaps a spouse
Or someone special—closer to our liking,
Wanting to be bound or unbound, figuring
And feigning what really counts in the bed
For winning or losing a battle in our head!

Busy or appearing to be busy in the office,
We play the game of survival with finesse
(Like children at school, cheating on tests).
Cussing, we push for political correctness.
With forked tongues we praise—to enthrall
And so deceive clients and customers and all.

Thus we impart some semblance of meaning
To our dross life of the American dreaming:
Sharpening our skills, most avidly advancing
Our information technology to divinely soar
Into a cloud of bells and whistles we so adore
To install in our lives for commerce's sake
And keep the social media constantly awake
To tune in all subjects, except the self we own.

Children are busy with video war games still,
Some unhappy runts devise ways to mass kill.
With our eyes focused on smart handy phones,
We absently walk and drive and talk all the more,
Praising electronic gadgets, including the drones,
To impress others—especially the Crescent choir,
For it helps prevent the *thinking* that we really require;
But leave it for the Silicon Valley guys to acquire.

03 54 80
Our Occupation

———————————— o ————————————

We open windows to let in the light
We light electric candles to see in the night
We go to the church to expiate our sin
We open our hearts to let others in
We knock on doors, wanting to be let in
We make a promise and keep it unbroken
We picture a world of peace and justice
We see necessity in this idea and practice
We respect life, liberty, and happiness

We work to remain in health and fitness
We don't like to remain static
We like all strains of art and music
We love playing and watching sports
We enjoy thrilling rides in cars and boats
We are kind to our cats and dogs
We are good at raising cows and hogs
We excel in science and technology
We have made great strides in cosmology

For all these virtues we make no apology
For we are Americans who love diversity

‹ 55 ›
Insensitivity

———————— o ————————

It is amazing!
        How can it be?
        That we are OK
        In our tragic loss,
        Feel no despair,
        Or even see
        That we are still
                There on the cross.

II

Our senses for sensing
        Were gifted by God
        Before Adam's fall,
        So why is our heart
        Insensitive and hard
        And our sharp mind
        Not so keen to hear
                Their urgent call?

III

Now our feelings
        For us and others
        Occupy a hard,
        Icy, cold center
        Of indifference
        That none bothers
        To melt or thaw,
                Lest a care may enter.

IV

Alas! we have sunk
      Deep into the earth,
      To crawl there with
      Slimy, blind worms,
      And just like them,
      Feeling no mirth,
      Nor sensing sorrow,
            We inanely spend our terms.

V

Insensitivity and indifference
      Have led us to shut
      Windows of our soul,
      Or, for some dole,
      To bargain with the devil
      In a Faustian fashion.
      We have sadly chosen
            To fall in a deep hole.

VI

O sweet oblivion!
      Go, drape us on
      With your thick
      Insensitive skin.
      Keep us etherized
      Until we are gone
      And are no more
            To rapture a kin.

ೞ 56 ೲ
Orphaned Child

───────── o ─────────

I saw her once—in a trance,
A sweet little girl—about ten,
Dancing bare feet in a cobbled street
Of a heavily shelled town in France.

The sun was high in the sky,
Pouring hot and heavy
Scorching rays on every stone and soul
Underfoot and nearby.

A throng of people—young and old,
In a circle—shuffling their feet,
Watched her perform in the dizzying heat,
A wild dance—for a sou or two sold.

The child kept hopping briskly on the street
To escape the beating heat,
Shaking her hands and hips in the thin air,
Just to disclaim her fear.

She turned and twisted—bent to please,
With starved guts in rhythmic tease.
The merciless sun paused in the sky blue
And dyed her hair an amber hue.

The dance took its own time and toll.
Some were moved to toss in a sou.
As the child picked the coins for her bread,
I saw the cobblestones smeared bloodred.

ༀ 57 ༃

Omen

─────────── o ───────────

A shooting star
Burning with passion,
Blazing the moonless night,
Slashed the slumbering sky;
Then quenched its passion
In the Aegean Sea.

Those who witnessed its demise
(After its brief meteoric rise)
Held their breath in surprise.
Helen saw in this an evil omen.
Shaken, she fell into the mighty arms
Of her lover—Paris, the prince of Troy.

They had come out to the beach,
For the Greeks had lifted the siege,
Leaving a wooden horse behind
To teach the unsuspecting Trojans
A lesson in the Greek treachery.
But Paris was blind to all tragedy.

He stretched out on the soft sand,
Pulling hesitant Helen to his side;
There he kissed her trembling lips
Sipping eagerly the oozing brine.
Oh, his lovemaking was intense
Like the light of an exploding star.

But Helen was distraught with panic.
In these omens she saw the fate of Troy:
Menelaus would surely return to claim her,

And the great House of Priam destroy.
Blood ran down the streets next day
And Homer's Helen
Was taken away.

ൟ 58 ൠ
A Live Shadow
———————————— o ————————————

The sun peeled a shadow off her face
And stamped it on a white marble wall
For the world its eloquent lines to trace
And find how history makes us recall
The reasons for our downfall.

In profile, the face was very refined,
With an uplifted brow—broadly wise,
The nose, lips, and chin well defined,
And a swan-neck pleasing to the eyes—
Lending the shadow no disguise.

The passersby who looked at the wall
And thereon saw etched a phantom face,
Wondered whose visage it was after all.
Was its live source nearby in place
Or floating somewhere in the space?

As the sun in the west was setting low,
A strange glow lighted up the shadow,
As if it were miraculously coming to life
And about to speak of her endured strife
In a time and place with mischief rife.

Murder of innocence, and of thought,
Followed by attempts at ethnic cleansing
Of those who were selectively caught,
Because their beliefs did not coincide
With those who had power to decide.

Slowly, the live shadow faced the crowd
And began to speak—like on the celluloid:
"My country was secular—and of it proud,
Where religious differences didn't colloid,
Nor were inter-alliances disallowed.

"But soon a wind of ethnic hatred blew,
That tore the old fabric of unity asunder;
The religious zealots, guns and sabers drew
To kill their 'enemies' or put them under,
Actually—for easy rape and plunder.

"Families and friends were split apart,
Age-old amity wrenched from their heart.
The women had to offer their naked bodies
To fill their swollen bellies or find ways
To reach other shores without delays.

"I was one of those who met this fate—
Separated from my mom, dad, and mate,
Found refuge in a cool, sheltering country,
Where I am accepted by all and sundry
And stand rooted as a sturdy oak tree."

Having said this, the picture faded away,
Leaving us deeply affected and thinking
About the wages of intolerance we pay
And the punishment we keep on taking,
For human destiny is of our own making.

⟨ 59 ⟩
Contradiction

─────────── o ───────────

She is against all
Forms of tyranny,
Including irony,
Except her own,
To which she ascribes,
By extension and *a priori*,
A noble intention *post priori*.

If asked to answer
An innocent question,
It is naked aggression
That must be quickly nipped,
Lest it becomes a contention
So unworthy, so unbecoming,
Of her attention—sitting or standing.

She is against
Bias and prejudice
For race, sex, age, or disability,
Practiced or weakly regulated;
But her heart is bent on rewarding
Those who have no cause or standing
If she finds they are in her political kettle
Or if her eyes on them amorously settle.

৵ 60 ৶
A Cry for Acceptance
―――――――――――― o ――――――――――――

Written after hearing a speech by Karen Van Fossan on
discrimination against sexual orientation, given at the
Unitarian Church in Bismarck, North Dakota

―――――――――――― o ――――――――――――

The tremulous pause before you spoke of raw injustice,
The silent prayer you made to gather poise and finesse,
The unshed tear shining in your eye as a diamond point
Awakened the assembled few to recognize and anoint
The victims of hate and hubris conjoint.

As you made the case against prejudice and naked terror
Unleashed on those innocent of any self-conceived error,
Tormented by slurs, slashed by daggers, dragged in mud,
Sharp anguish ripped through the crowd; tears were shed
To wash the lingering stains of blood.

The men or women who find comfort in their own kind
And like to love and live together in a union so maligned
By the self-righteous, primitive hordes pose no real threat
To the society or state, or ever make our good God shut
The doors of mercy on those who are differently cut.

Natural variance and struggle for survival raise this voice:
Claims of superiority in color, form, function, or choice
Rest, verily, on hollow rocks of conceit and blind belief.
Only you can bring some hope, reason, and needed relief
To those who watch in disbelief.

☙ 61 ❧
Mourning
———————————— ο ————————————

It kept on coming from that open window!
On the third floor of the apartment complex
Facing mine, across the derelict lane:
A groaning sound—like persistent moaning—
Each spell extending in a droning noise,
Seemingly from a sick old woman in pain.

I wondered if she was attended to or all alone.
This cry of anguish drove me insane.
I shut my window to muffle the sound,
But it buzzed in my head round and round.

And I couldn't take it anymore.
So I walked out of my apartment door,
Bent on doing something in this regard:
I knew not what, but it hit me hard
To be reminded how miserable life can be
As we get old and find ourselves so lonely.

Getting old is on everybody's plate,
But loneliness is a curse of fate;
It devours your life faster than you can see
A fish gobbling your proffered bait.

This teeming world is a very lonely place
To many men and women who can't face
Differences in opinion, religion, or race,
Or different expressions of sex or age.
Yet we can't keep on ignoring forever
Our common needs that bind us together.

So I sped quickly to the other building
And met the apartment manager in his office.
He said, "Yes, an old woman lived in that unit,
Alone with her golden retriever—crazy a bit.
But she died yesterday, and since then her dog
Has been mourning—piteously groaning."

‍ 62 ‍

The Fruit of Sin

———————— o ————————

The air in the Great Hall was heavy with grief.
    It crawled on the floor in eerie swirls.
    It clung to the columns in creepy curls.
All assembled there were staring in disbelief.

Sitting motionless on the hardwood chairs
    Around a coffin, wherein lay the cold
    Body of a woman—twenty years old,
The mourners were holding back their tears.

She had died in sleep of an unknown cause.
    The few who seemingly knew her well
    Couldn't, for shock or fear, see or tell
What the cause of her untimely death was.

None of them but one knew for sure
    Whence and why she had come there,
    But they weren't dumb or lacking care
Not to sense she was stricken and poor.

Ms. Lisa had come from a big metropolis.
    She was a front teller in a high-rise bank,
    Good at numbers, also fearless and frank,
With no idea she would end up in a necropolis.

She had come in search of a former lover,
    Who had embezzled from his workplace
    And was now in this town, hiding his face
After making her pregnant in his bower.

The wicked lover saw Lisa in his pursuit,
    Trailing him to this out-of-the-way town.
    Sensing arrest, he so feared for his crown
And planned to snuff her out—like a brute.

One night he went to her rented quarter,
    Begging her forgiveness on his two knees,
    Gaining her trust with his faked apologies.
But the wretch was planning her murder.

After making up with a few nice words said,
    Poor Lisa fell asleep on the rumpled bed.
    He placed a pillow on her upturned head
And with demonic force choked her dead.

He wasn't troubled by this dastardly act,
    But emboldened to play it out to the hilt.
    To divert public attention from his guilt,
He anonymously called the police to react.

The authorities found Lisa dead in her room,
    With no definite clues that would lead
    To the person who committed this deed—
Save a coat button in the bristles of a broom.

Lisa's body was placed in the Hall for a reason:
    To see if her wily killer was still around,
    And if lured, he could be so easily bound;
For a criminal betrays himself in due season.

So Lisa's killer too went to the Great Hall,
    Pretending cleverly to be a deeply caring soul,
    Hiding his identity like an embedded mole,
But he couldn't keep up this masquerade at all.

For a button was missing on the culprit's coat.
 The rest were similar to one they had found
 At the scene of crime; so he was duly bound
For questioning and found guilty by the court.

This story was related to me by a friend of mine
 Who was a fine police detective in his time
And by effort and luck solved many a crime.
He concluded: "Adam's progeny is not that fine."

Adding, "We are the inheritors of a hungry knife,
Wielded first by Abraham on his own son
 To gain favor in the eyes of the Great One;
This curse assumes many forms in our selfish life."

I told my friend, "This analogy doesn't fit the story."
 He answered, "Love's fruit isn't always sweet,
 Like the apple of Eden's tree, we mustn't eat,
And if we do, we do surely provoke God's fury."

❧ 63 ❧
Pearls of Friendship

───────────── o ─────────────

When you laid your pearls in front of my eyes,
String by string, with a soft glow and a smile,
Each unique, yet each with pearls of the same size,
I heard you both, as it were, from a distant isle,
Talking as Neptune's daughters, to my surprise,
Of ideas in verses that render substance to style.

The pearls spoke mutely of their radiant beauty,
Granted them by the deep ocean and the clam.
You radiated your impeccable self with plenty
Of poise, coming from an awareness of "I Am"
That brings one closer to truth and humanity,
Like rain, rivulets, and streams rush to fill a dam.

The luster of some personalities can't hide—
Be it a cloudy, rainy, or dreary day at work.
Standing by a counter or hidden under a lid,
Neither you nor the pearls can one dare shirk,
For that would demean elegance, God forbid,
And make the good-intentioned person a jerk.

Your emphatic call to form a vernal fellowship
Is a soothing idea and accepted with gratitude;
For there may grow a shiny pearl of friendship,
Just as a fading rose—growing in its certitude
Of life's brevity—sees beauty in a bee's kinship
And thus frees itself of the thorns of solitude.

ॐ 64 ॐ
To Stephen D. Merrill
──────────── ○ ────────────

Sweet are the pleasures that to verse belong,
And doubly sweet a brotherhood in song.
—John Keats
──────────── ○ ────────────

My dear friend, Doc Stephen,
I'm blessed in your friendship,
Which began a long time ago
In a college town in Colorado,
Where our views found a kinship.

We were there for a meeting
Focused on land and crop sciences,
Going over new ideas and advances,
But, learning more while eating
At the funky Bottoms Up Diner,
Where the fare was quite delicious
And our conversation sumptuous.
Nothing else could have been finer.

Moving from subject to subject,
We chewed on some philosophies,
Social and political controversies,
Without a specific aim or object.
Thus discovering mutual interests,
We developed a lasting friendship
That neither imposed any hardship
Nor turned us into crazy sophists.

Then, in North Dakota, life was easy:
You working for the Big Brother
And I for another—a lot smaller—

But both in Land Reclamation busy.
Your wedge plots at Center and Stanton
Yielded information that helped change
The state's reclamation rules—to manage
The replacement of soil on the overburden.

Your interest in saving the environment
From misuse—out of greed we betray—
Still continues in your own charming way
And fills me with pure amazement.
There are other passions too that stir you:
Foreign languages, cultures, and faces,
Which beckon you to far-flung places,
Since all forms of prejudice you eschew.

There came to us a time of adventure
When we traveled through teeming India,
The land of Rama, Krishna, and Buddha,
Where diverse races and faiths anchor
Their hopes in freedom and democracy,
Based on the principles of Dharma yoga
And the belief in the power of karma
That led to their intellectual aristocracy.

Remember the places and people we saw,
The research and admin centers, as they go,
The lust for life carved in stones at Khajuraho,
The turbaned tribals pulling on a hookah,
My nephew's wedding with a cute doctor
Clad in fine silks, smiles, and laughter,
Our reception and presentations at the HAU,
And the majestic Taj Mahal's incredible view.

As the years have bleached our heads,
The brotherly affection we have shown
Has spread its strong roots and grown,

Connecting our lives and family threads.
But there is so much more to this story:
For there are so many virtues I have seen
In you, Steve, which a world to me mean.
Had I some, it would add to our glory.

෫ 65 ෩
Reminiscent

———————————— o ————————————

She is an auditory expert,
Well versed in sensory art,
But when I saw her first,
From both near and afar,
She faintly reminded me of
An exceptional work of art.

She seemed to have alighted
Softly from a museum wall
And is now working in a hall
Where patients are delighted
To see that their dim hearing
Can be cured easily, after all.
In a white lab coat walks she,
But I wonder who it could be.

She has an enigmatic smile
And a dreamy, distant gaze
(That artists like to capture)
And throws you into a maze
Of high-tech auditory-exam
In her clinic's cloistered isle.
She keeps the record on file
To get a full sensory picture.

Now it suddenly comes to me
That in her face and art
Is a semblance of a sort
Of a Florentine thought:
In Nicole, *Mona Lisa* you see,
In her scientific art, da Vinci.

α 66 ജ
Mirage

_____ o _____

When shallow waters are deemed too darn deep,
And the nanny goats are mistaken for woolly sheep,
The watchdogs are taking a deep, oblivious sleep.

When mere shadows are seen as solid substance,
And important decisions are made in an instance,
The watchdogs are looking from a foggy distance.

When dream castles are built out of crystal sand,
And water lilies are planted on the arid highland,
The watchdogs are dancing crazy in a merry band.

When justice is paid a glossy painted lip service,
And the bureaucratic tape binds each in its service,
The watchdogs are busy doing a great disservice.

When the selfish rich ride the horse named Charity,
And dancing showgirls reveal much in sheer clarity,
The watchdogs can't help but become openly flirty.

When a lusty jackass can't get a good night's rest
And wanders from bed to bed as a pesky love pest,
The watchdogs are also taking turns in this quest.

ಇ 67 ಉ
Magic Chef

———————————— o ————————————

You are a skilled chopper and dicer
Of onion, garlic, celery, and cicer.
You're a magic chef—a gourmet kaiser.

You know how to neatly spice a dish,
Be it of veggies, mutton, beef, pork, or fish.
You're a magic chef—hard to vanquish.

You prefer using spices from the East:
Coriander, cumin, and ginger, at least.
You're a magic chef—a turmeric artiste.

You don't like the Italian flavors to bypass:
Basil, rosemary, oregano, and lemongrass.
You are a magic chef, admired by every lass.

You serve truth with a touch of lime.
You roast lies with a dash of thyme.
You're, indeed, a magic chef sublime.

You toss exotic condiments with finesse,
Cinnamon, cardamom, nutmeg to caress.
You're a magic chef who truly pleases us.

☙ 68 ❧

Go South

―――――○―――――

Oh!
Let us go
To the south,
To the warm south,
Where the sun hangs low
And the ocean breeze
Blows with ease
As we go.

Oh!
Let us go
To the south,
To the balmy south,
Where red clouds break
Into rain and flow
Slowly below
To slake.

Oh!
Let us go
To the south,
To the exotic south,
Where love is in the air,
With its fragrance
Everywhere,
My dear.

Oh!
Let us go
To the south,
To the magical south,

Where a fantastic altitude
To Gabriel's Realism
Was attained in
Solitude.

ೞ 69 ೞ
COVID-19

———————————— o ————————————

Come closer to me tonight,
Hold me to your heart with no fright
Of the viral pandemic we have seen
Now sweeping us away for months
With the horrible spikes of COVID-19,
Which the world had never seen.

Sleep by my side all night
Without closing your eyes
Until the sun's glowing corona
Warmly into our chamber flies
Chasing away the dread virus
From our frightened lives.

I will press you to my face
Without my hideous mask
Hoping you too will unmask
And daringly this idea embrace.
We have kept a distance of six feet
And for months avoided to meet.

COVID-19 has scared the world,
Making our passions fall apart,
Not to speak of the millions lost
In their struggle for a breath to last.
It is time we invent that vaccine
Whose power can be assuredly seen.

We must also our love engines start
Before our minds deathward lean.
So, my brave darling, be not afraid,
No matter where we have been—

Months of fear, dread and isolation,
Lock downs, masks and, distancing,
Hand washing and sanitizing, collapsing
Economy and health-care industry,
political bickering and uncertainty—
Shattering our age-old certainty.

௰ 70 ௺
Learn from Regret

─────────── 0 ───────────

I

How soon we forget
Remorse and regret!
And fall back again
In the same old rut
Of loving and hating,
Baiting and cheating.

II

Then, finding a way
To peacefully lay
Down our conscience
By faking penitence,
Calling it repentance
To gain acceptance.

III

This—a sly technique
Is, indeed, so unique!
For it easily redeems
Us in our own eyes
And the clergy guys'.
Never mind who lies!

V

Remorse would help
Save us from ourselves,
Only if it stays with us
To infuse and harness
The wisdom we need
And must always heed.

VI

It will not let us repeat
The mistakes that beat
Us over and over again,
And our strength drain.
So learn from remorse,
For it is a rich resource.

VII

Then we will not regret
Once again or ever fret
In choosing our friends,
Lovers, words, or trends;
For in our past remorse,
We find the right course,

IV

Forgetting your sins
Is like storing in bins
The trash you owned,
But never ever let go.
It'll keep on growing,
As grass after mowing.

VIII

Which is smarter to take
Than tempting a snake,
Whose sexy-vexy form
Would do us great harm.
So reject but don't forget
Past remorse and regret.

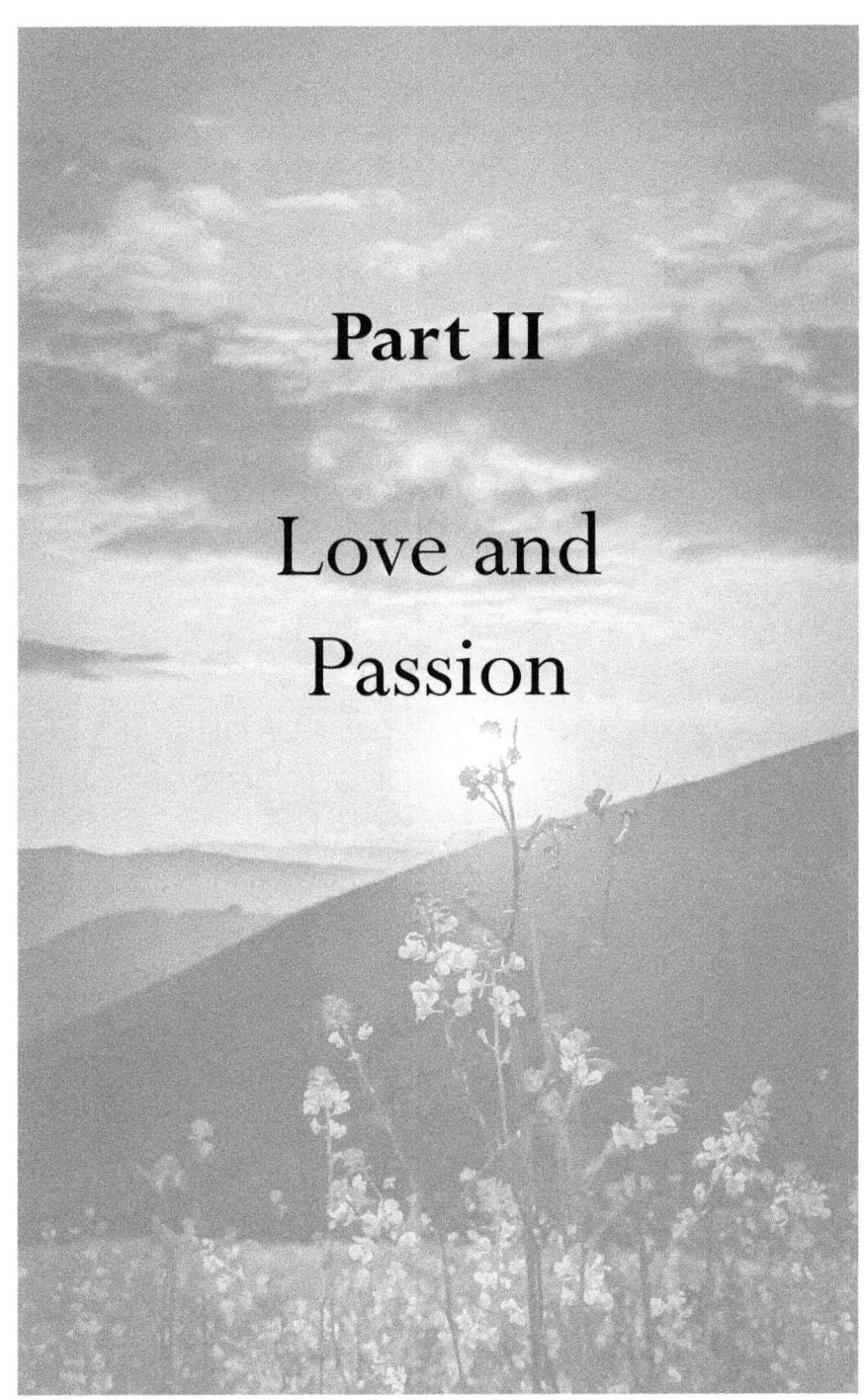

Part II

Love and Passion

Love and Passion

The greatest pleasure of life is love.
—Euripedes

Love is the name for our pursuit
of wholeness, for our desire
to be complete.
—Plato

Only Passions, great passions,
can elevate the soul to great things.
—Denis Diderot

☙ 71 ❧
Love's Abode

———— o ————

Is it in the heart
Or in the mind where
Love dwells? Or there
In the soul, as "thou art"?

Love, your forms are infinite
In your purpose, shape, and scope;
You dwell in the quark and string
The universe in its manifest hope.

You dwell in the blades of grass,
In the shrubs and trees that pass
Your grandeur in rich showers
Of color and scent of flowers.

You are in the mother's milk,
In the morphed cocoon of silk.
You are on the lips of an infant
And in the eyes of a supplicant.

You are in the innocent smile,
As rays of light with no guile.
You shine in the morning dew,
And the tear dropped for you.

You are in the core of a stone
And on the wings of a tide and tone.
All things inanimate or animate,
Rich or poor, find you incarnate.

Incarnate in them, within and around.
You suffuse each and then surround,
Leaving no space or second untouched,
No thought or act—fetched or unfetched.

Though readily visible is your face
In the lovers' kiss and embrace,
Allow us to see clearly your real charm
In its supreme singularity and divine form.

ை 72 ௸
Feeling Your Presence

From the falling leaves of autumn,
Landing to warm the Mother Earth,
With their soft hugs and kisses,
Came the sound of your breathing.

A gentle breeze blew through the trees,
Caressing their bare, trembling arms,
Calming the fear of coming injuries
From the sharp white fangs of winter.

The feeble sun was about to disappear
Behind the distant mountain peaks,
Making its way through the red clouds
Reluctantly—wanting to keep on shining.

Plaintive notes of a flute came from afar,
Announcing the approaching feet of Night—
A mysterious, veiled lady dressed in black,
Whispering sweetly to close our eyes.

All this was unfolding before my eyes
When a hand softly touched my shoulder;
I turned around and saw my Love smiling
And breathing gently—

Like the leaves I had seen falling from the trees,
Like the breeze caressing their trembling arms,
Like the notes of the flute coming from afar,
Like the veiled lady kissing us good night.

⚂ 73 ⚃
My Love

──────────── o ────────────

As the sun brings the day to my door
In warm waves of light and much more;
As the moon casts shadows on the floor,
Touching my mortal frame to explore;
You, my love, reach deep into my soul,
With unsaid words scoring their goal.

You speak with eyes that shine, as before,
Of love that binds soul to soul and more.
And in purest form is bound to adore
All in close kinship with God at its core.
Yes, my darling, you awakened my soul
By a look in your eyes adorned with kohl.

Your generous gift of love and friendship,
Your gorgeous charm and gentle kinship,
Your ceaseless caring and selfless sharing,
Your joys and fears quite readily nearing,
Fill your eyes with warm mist and rain,
Washing away all my life's pain and strain.

But now I'm sitting here all alone,
Thinking of how fast our time has flown.
Your each soulful gesture remains alive,
Giving me will and strength to survive.
Wherever I go, I see and carry your light—
As the sun in the day and moon in the night.

❦ 74 ❧
I Love You

———— ○ ————

How do I love thee? Let me count the ways.
I love thee to the depth and breadth and height
My soul can reach, when feeling out of sight
For the ends of being and ideal Grace.
—Elizabeth Barrett Browning, "Sonnet XLIII"

———— ○ ————

I want to hold you tenderly in my gaze,
Through the spring thaws and summer blaze,
From violet dusk to golden dawn, and on and on,
Until my heart is at rest and I am gone.

Touch your face and trace your flitting shadow
In the west wind—stirring petals in the meadow
Or stand on life's shore to own one more wave—
So I too am born again with the love you gave.

Feel your sweet breath in my veins, stimulating
My senses and soul, a single cool-flame making;
Your passionate promises make me live and bold
And happily cast me in their enchanting mold.

Drink the cup of life sweetened by your song
Of love and light, with wisdom teaming along,
That you sing gracefully with heavenly charm
And draw all my senses to your earthly form.

From dust to flesh and from flesh back to dust,
Only hope remains, which too may rot or rust;
For bound we are to unending cycles of change,
But love alone saves life from being too strange.

෦ 75 ෨
Flowers

Fresh-cut flowers
In a crystal vase
Standing at a table
Adorn her face.

When I walk in
Through the patio door
With my eyes on the floor,
I look up with anticipation:

And see her there
Sitting in a chair
At the far end of the table
—In her sable—
Staring at the vase.
Partly hiding is her face
Behind the flowers,
Looking like one of them.

Drawn by the rich colors
Of all the fragrant flowers,
I approach timidly—to kiss,
And see an iris in her iris.

❧ 76 ❧
The Seasons of Love

———————— ◇ ————————

I
Spring

Daffodils arrived in the morning,
Suddenly announcing spring;
Cool-scented air filled the valley below
The mountains, still capped with snow,
Reflecting the golden glow of the morning sun.

Your hazel eyes caught the tender
Gleam of a long-forgotten dream
And opened wide in surprise;
The daffodil stood before you as a bride,
Touching your face with love and pride.

II
Summer

In the sumptuous heat of the midday sun,
Summer arrived with a warm breeze.
Swarms of humming bees are kissing the flowers
Joyously, sipping their nectar with artful ease.
The bees are happy, rid of winter freeze.

You're standing in a chemise over the breast.
Pearls of sweat adorn your neck and chest.
A sensuous fragrance surrounds your body.
The summer haze works in strange ways,
Reminding you of the joys of bygone days.

III
Autumn

Autumn entered at dusk with bushels of grain.
The trees are heaving under the ripening strain
Of pears, apples, and apricots—ready to be sold.
The leaves are turning purple, red, and gold.
The nights are beginning to feel pleasantly cold.

Your face is framed in curls of flaming hair,
The autumn breeze blowing it here and there.
A faint smile lights up your eyes,
Hiding a sweet secret memory behind the veil.
Yes, a tender, loving time must now prevail.

IV
Winter

Lo! the night has fallen in a heap of snow;
dancing flakes are crowding the turbid sky.
Soon icy winds will blow high and low.
Crackling fires are lit in the fireplaces,
Warming the loving hearts in right places.

You are looking through a frosted pane,
Wondering when he will appear in your lane,
Hold you in a warm embrace, and kiss your face.
Lo and behold! He is at your door, ready to enter
The home of his dreams—your heart's center.

ભ 77 ৯

The Soul Mate

When I was in the saddle of my youth,
Surrounded by comfort and plentitude,
Cherishing books, fine foods, and friends,
Enjoying all the in-fashion trends,
Only one thing vexed my attitude:
The absence of a soul mate in my life.

I hadn't seen her earthly form before,
But her spirit was knocking at my door.
I searched for her in the human streams
As she kept on appearing in my dreams.
This tension stretched me day by day
As her soul in my heart dormant lay.

Then, one day, I saw her face-to-face
At a mutual friend's place.
She was standing in a corner of the room;
One look at her banished my gloom.
She introduced herself with a knowing smile;
Time sped backward on the clock's dial:

My past came back to me.
At the far end of time's tunnel stood she;
We were only specks of consciousness then,
In the universe of being and becoming, when
The souls wandered in search of each other
To fulfill God's design of bringing them together.

ೞ 78 ೲ
Beholden

———— o ————

To you, my love, I am most beholden,
As the rainbow is to its father golden,
As the stream to its preserving banks
And its solid bed and verdurous flanks;
Without you, I wouldn't be.

You have brought sunshine in my life,
Helped me cope with all my strife,
Taught me to read between the lines,
To discover the real meaning of signs;
Without you, I wouldn't know

That there is a garden within our soul,
And its cultivation should be our goal.
If we want to see and smell the flowers,
We must prove to be faithful lovers;
Without you, it wouldn't be so.

For time stands still in your embrace.
Sunshine illumines a desire in your face,
Filling my heart and quickening its pace.
Uncertainty vanishes with God's grace;
Without you, it wouldn't be true.

When we hold each other tenderly
And make our desires known honestly,
Their fulfillment presents no difficulty.
The garden in our soul has this faculty;
With you, all my dreams come true.

൦൴ 79 ൵൦
Your Smile

———————— o ————————

Your smile is like the unfolding of a flower
After the morning fog and a gentle shower,
Leaving behind the sparkling diamond dew
On the petals, as on your lips painted anew.

Your smile is like a perfumed ocean breeze,
Blowing at night through the jasmine trees,
Providing relief from the wearing hot day
To those who can't sleep or mindfully pray.

Your smile is like a rising crescent moon
Playing with her starry friends that swoon
At her majestic glide through the night sky,
Bringing an acute desire in the lover's eye.

Your smile is like a cup of sparkling wine
That bubbles with life and invites to dine
At a well-laid table in the restaurant grand,
With music pouring from a lively band.

Your smile is like the recurring dream
That beckons me, like the lighthouse beam,
To come ashore from the sea of my despair
And hold you close, so that our hearts repair.

✿ 80 ✿
Dreamed Ecstasy
— o —

I am trying to recall
A half-remembered dream
But can't piece it together all,
For time is a fast-flowing stream.

We were reposing on its bank,
In the tall green clumpy grass,
Seasonally thick and rank,
Eyeing the bridge that reached across.

The waters crashed on the boulders,
Rousing passion in the stream;
We clasped each other's shoulders,
Thrilled by the tossed spray and steam.

It fogged the banks and our brains,
Pressing us to be nearer and nearer,
Melding into one, releasing the reins
That had kept us from being closer.

It was like a dream fulfilled,
Long abandoned to the subconscious,
Where it was held choked and stilled;
Of this pain we were fully conscious.

Lying there in the tall grass
That afternoon, with sun piercing the mist,
Casting a rainbow on my lovely lass—
I now recall: we more than simply kissed.

℃ 81 ℈
The Blue Lake

———————————— ० ————————————

I remember the Blue Lake
As vividly as your eyes:
Both too deep to fathom,
Both reflecting the blue skies.

We used to stroll on its shore,
Hand in hand, trying to explore
The depth of our feelings
That stirred our heart and soul.

Like the lake, your blue eyes
Couldn't see or surmise!
The fluttering of my heart—
Hushed by the wings of thought.

Neither could I make out
From your unwrinkled brow:
What were you thinking about
Whenever I touched a vein of love.

Then, one day, we set up a tent
On the lake's western front,
And therein a blissful night spent,
Unleashing a flood of feelings…
With our lips locked, our hearts
Spoke in the bare dialect of love.
We lay down together, holding
Each other in undressed ecstasy.

I saw the soul of the Blue Lake
Snugly dwelling in your eyes;
You felt sure—there in your heart:
That we could now a new life start.

ೞ 82 ೞ
The Astral Dance

—————————— o ——————————

The horned owl
Calls me in the nights:
To come out in the cold
And watch the Northern Lights.

I try to leave my warm bed,
But a strong silky thread
Tied to the horns of love,
Holds me down in its prow.

I love watching the Northern Lights,
But I also like to make love;
So I light a candle bright
And watch her dance all night.

The Northern lights ignite
Sparks down my spine,
But so does the shimmering sight
Of my lady from the Nordic alpine.

Moments gobble up time
In wee fractions of space!
And I sit there in a trance
Watching this twin astral dance.

෬ 83 ๖෭

Your Love Dance

———————————— o ————————————

O, learn to love, the lesson is but plain,
And once made perfect, never lost again.
—William Shakespeare, *Venus and Adonis*

———————————— o ————————————

You love with a heart wild with desire;
It shows in every dancing step you take.
I am carried away by your hidden fire;
It lifts me higher for your and my sake,
Allowing us both to touch the rainbow
Arching the heavens in a colorful show.
As my arms circle your waist, sparks fly.

Your lovely eyes catch the golden glare
Of Apollo, rising from his restful sleep,
Then reflect it with a jaunty flare.
This amazing spark you admirably keep,
With all the play and wisdom combined
That the gods on anyone shined.
In your eyes, many colors of love I find.

In the evenings, when the fiery hot sun
Eases into the cool bosom of the blue sea,
Painting the horizon in crimson and dun,
You let your red locks down to hold me,
By the tendrils of an amber vine treading,
My heart's chambers threading—silently;
You know the passion it kindles in me!

As the evening greets the promising night,
After a repast of delicious food and drink,
You and I curl together as we fancy right,

Without letting our lighted senses blink.
For the night is still young and yearning
To learn more from each other's turning;
I fulfill your needs, and you do mine.

Your love dance is not of the usual kind,
Neither blindly physical nor etherized,
But graced with a movement so refined
That it appears to be divinely actualized,
Lifting us both up into the ethereal skies
Where love's pure ecstasy fills our eyes,
Making us see: love-making is divine.

You love with all your body, mind, and soul,
A gift given to you by gods, as Venus was;
But you make your Adonis bold and whole,
Letting him shed his coyness for the cause.
No mortal woman has easily gained this art,
Unless she was some god's consort.
I gratefully thank the gods, for you are mine.

ℭℛ 84 ℬℭ
Passion

─────── ○ ───────

As you approach me in your armed splendor,
Aiming your barbed spear at my heart's chamber,
I tremble timorously in much-awaited delight;
My heart leaps forth with no trace of fright.

Love, my sweet enemy, you are ready to invade
The core of my being, yet I mustn't stop or evade
You with my hesitance, but yield my ground
Before your passion is spent and ecstasy found.

Allow me first to assemble my bearing and breath
To make your victory worth your quick death,
Which surely you shall find in my mortal embrace;
So, why not call on eternity to save your face.

But if you insist on taking me in your own way,
Be ready to draw my virgin blood—that wager I lay.
Think twice before your desires overflow the dam,
For love and passion must evenly mix and flow.

I'm eager and ready to dance with you, my love,
If you only wait awhile and see how and why
It must begin and end in ecstasy, not in sorrow.
Come again in splendor and wake me tomorrow.

෬ 85 ෬
Afraid to Admit Love

———————————— o ————————————

Thank you, my friend, for staying in touch;
I won't say much, but surely this much:
You kept your feelings from crossing the line
Teaching me also how to restrain mine.

In this manner, we remained tongue-tied
For too long, no matter how hard we tried
To open our dammed-up beating hearts
That we've bravely tied in Gordian knots.

You're a fast river hugging both banks
But I'm the one who grudgingly thanks
Even when your rapid flow erodes my side
Causing it to crumble and slide,
Which I'm compelled to bravely hide.

Oh there is so much we hide from each other!
Yet we keep on whispering together
Under a gently falling rain
That neither slakes us nor drowns our pain.

We wish each other happy days and seasons!
Hardly ever giving sufficient reasons
For sharing a joyous occasion in absentia,
As if we're draped in vestures of dementia.

We laugh at each other's texted jokes!
Which break our hearts with heavy strokes.
Why do we constantly keep pretending,
And dolefully refrain from our needs attending?

Perhaps, *we are* afraid of our dark shadows!

ᴄ᷈ 86 ᴐ᷈
A Small Favor

—— o ——

Sleep comes and goes
While I struggle on the divan
With the demons of temptation;
Holding an empty glass
—Calling it half-full—
Feeling the tug and pull.

She is standing nearby,
Hiding her uncontrollable yawns
With hands pressed against her lips.
We are awaiting the dawn.
Red wine has risen to her eyes.
In the bedroom the baby cries.

I am feeling restless
To leave for my home.
But "Stay, stay," she cries,
"There's a thing I have to show."
So what should I do?
My curiosity grows too.

She goes into the bedroom, then
Shows up in a transparent gown,
Revealing her just-suckled breasts.
She plops on the divan next to me,
Then aggressively pulls me over,
Begging me to stay, and stay all night…

My eyes look deep into her eyes,
We are caught in a net of surprise.
She guides my hand to her thighs
And saturates the air with her sighs.
Soon the walls echo our ecstatic cries
And our welded being melts and dies.

ल 87 ॐ
A Sonnet

———————— o ————————

You awaken the coiled serpent
Of hot desire in my breast!
When you come naked to my bed
And lay your head on my chest.
The dry brambles of my thought
Are then suddenly set on fire,
And I am transformed into a satyr.
You catch me floating in the air,
And pull me down to eagerly sip
The nectar from your spring fair.
I bury my soul in the moist earth
Of the valley beneath the twin hills;
You hold me there with your hands
Until the fair lady wills.

ༀ 88 ༀ
Partner Preference
— o —

She said "She was waiting
for you anxiously all night
with her restless eyes
burning holes in the ceiling
turning them only to see
why the door creaked
why the window rattled
hoping it was you.

"She had set the network
of her nerves in commotion
for fueling her passion
as she was vainly hoping
(perhaps, to herself joking)
this would be the night of nights
when your love for her would overflow
and the two of you would make it glow."

But she didn't know
you were with me
giving and receiving
deepest love and pleasure
from every inch of your body
from every recess of my mind
from the very depths of our soul
feeling secure in your masculinity
whose ability is well known to me.

So when you slipped into her bed
—pretending to be dead—
there was nothing she could do
except scream, "Damn you!"

ಆ 89 ಋ
A Tribute to You
―――――――――――――――― o ――――――――――――――――

How can your charm ever so fade
When all this at your feet is laid:
A heart full of love and adoration,
A head bowing low in admiration?

My eyes catch a fleeting shadow:
You! amid lilies in the meadow,
Where butterflies seem confused
By the heavenly scent so diffused.

Love, time has no power over you,
For he too is so captivated by you
And slows down his steeds to see
Which celestial being it could be!

Is it Diana, Minerva, or Olympia?
One or all! Singing in symphonia,
Playing under the pale olive trees,
Feeding sweet music to the breeze.

Oh! for a woman to be gods' worthy,
She must be celestial; but, if earthy,
She must surpass others in beauty,
Charm, and wit in measures plenty.

Since you are earthy, full of charm,
With lively wit and wisdom warm,
Spread your fiery wings like a lark,
And fly high to catch Apollo's spark.

Or, better, return my love as before;
I promise I'll cherish you even more
than the gods whom you so adore—
From a long-deserted, foggy shore.

෩ 90 ෫
Trust Yourself

———————————— o ————————————

I didn't come here merely
    To show you my face,
But to behold you tenderly
    And converse—face to face.

Your brow is high and wide,
    Holding back a noble thought.
Your eyes some secrets hide,
    But they quietly touch my heart.

Your cheeks are softly uplifted
    As seen in Inner Mongolia;
Your face is divinely gifted
    With sweet aura of magnolia.

Your almond eyes hold a mellow gaze—
    Full of compassion for all life,
Just like the Buddha in his days—
    Teaching how to banish all strife.

Your bosom has firm conviction:
    Love is another name of God;
So it must be full of passion—
    When you are serving the Lord.

I know you are fully conscious
    Of these gifts bestowed on you.
So, please don't ever be anxious
    Or doubt my admiration of you.

ೞ 91 ೞ
Where Your Beauty Lies

———————— o ————————

Where shall your beauty go
      When you're near sixty or so?
You look still quite youthful;
      I am being absolutely truthful.
Be not afraid to hear me say
      What I have enjoyed each day
That tied our past to future,
      As I see it happening in nature.

Your smooth and silky hair,
      With which you deftly snare;
Your cool, unwrinkled brow,
      Touching the clouds above;
Your shy emerald-green eyes,
      Where your real power lies;
Your sweet lips painted red,
      Which invite me to the bed;
Your smooth alabaster skin,
      Whose luster makes heads spin;
Your bare, sloping shoulders,
      Which pure admiration spur;
Your divinely shaped breasts,
      All my attention arrest;
Your tapered waist to pelvis,
      Draped in an exquisite challis—

All these marvelous attributes,
  Which garner many tributes,
Will progressively fade away;
  But my love will not decay,
For I wasn't merely interested
  In your bodily charms listed,
But in the beauty of your mind
  And soul that always shined.

☙ 92 ❧
A Caring Heart
— o —

Hard and heavy was the sound of silence
Inside my house when I heard someone
At my door. It had snowed fitfully
All day long, painting the place hoar.
I got up from my recliner—feeling sore
All over my body—and opened the door.
I saw my neighbor standing there in cold
Her visit at that late hour seemed too bold.

I let her in, asking what could I do for her.
She replied in a cold yet controlled voice,
"I have a question and nothing more."
She repeated this line with passion twice.
I realized she was angry and frustrated,
          but didn't understand why!
And I saw tears welling up in her eyes.
She wiped them off quickly, and demanded:

"Why didn't you let me know
Of your suffering and pain?"
Then she turned her back on me,
Sobbing quietly to my utter surprise.
I didn't know her well or long enough
As she had moved recently into a house
Next to mine, and I had once stopped
There to welcome her as a neighbor.

I gently asked her, "Why are you crying?"
She did not reply but sat down on a chair
To collect and calm herself from despair.
I offered her a glass of water and waited

For a while before I repeated my question.
She quietly replied, "I had a brother
Who looked just like you, but he died
On a wintry night because of my neglect."

I said, "I am terribly sorry, but how!"
She replied, "He was fighting cancer,
Battling severe pain and uncertainty,
And I was taking care of him at home.
One night I was out with my boyfriend,
Got home late and found my brother
Dead in his cruel bed. I can't get
That picture out of my head.

"A neighbor here told me that you too
Are suffering cancer and its vicious pain;
So I couldn't hold back from helping you,
For I can't this time let myself be absent gain."

ය 93 හ
Competition

───── o ─────

When my fellow poet,
Gulzaar, heard from me
That you, my sweetest Love,
Want to have a cup of tea
(No, not one but three!)
Together with him and me;
He watched my face to see,
How could I, not missing a beat,
With your desire so easily comply!

Hiding the color of rose
That quickly rose to my face,
I to my friend replied:
"My Love is not cruel but too kind;
She wants you in a circle
Your poems to recite,
So that she can find
Which one of us truly excels
In meter and rhyme."

He said, "I admire your bravery,
Both, towards her and me,
But how can you pretend
Not being envious of her 'Truly'?"
To this poisoning arrow

I calmly replied:
"Even Arjuna,[1] the greatest archer,
Had his moments of uncertainty,
But she is as noble as Draupadi."[2]

Oh, hear now what else it proves!
Holding me captive to her virtues:
She is vibrant as roses in full bloom,
One look at her dispels my gloom;
The light shining in her ebony eyes
Melts away the clouds in my skies
Her cute lips mint words of gold
That give me strength to hold
My life from fading away.

---

1 Pāndava hero in *Mahabharata* who won Draupadi
2 Wife of the five Pandeva brothers in the *Mahabharata*

❧ 94 ❧
Love and Freedom

———————————— o ————————————

As the morning freeze on the windshield
To the warming breeze does easily yield,
So shall the chill that weakens our will
Thaw when your voice the void shall fill.

The space stretched betwixt you and me
Is a fine fabric whose knots we can't see
Or untie; they're elastic bonds of love,
Which unite us and set us free somehow.

Love binds one to another, freeing each
Of isolation and despair, so we can reach
That place of freedom, which gives hope
Its wings to uplift life to its fullest scope.

Love asks none to set aside or surrender
Their identity or free will, or to render
Service burdensome to one or the other,
But fills their space with joy and wonder.

Yet there are those who define freedom
In terms of its ability to dispel boredom
By allowing them to sleep with anyone;
But is it freedom or a devouring demon?

So, my darling, thaw your frosty silence.
Let your thoughts pour out in a balance,
And define your desire with some clarity;
For freedom-giving love is not so flirty.

LaDonna

It is hard to remember
All the nuances and niceties
Of a bygone life—half spent in sleep.

Each night swallowed
The preceding day's toils and troubles
Sleeping in her welcoming arms—in peace.

Her sweet breath perfumed
The darkness of each night in the room
Where we slept without fear or gloom.

The sleeping heads
Woke up every morning to resume
The same old chores the day light consume.

The disquiet of day's labor
Made me hate the sunlight—not for melanoma,
But for the pleasure of sleeping with LaDonna.

O LaDonna! Where are you?
Now that I am laid off—to avoid corona
We could have doubled our sleep and kama.[1]

---

1   Sexual pleasure

ଓ୪ 96 ଓଡ
Pursuit

———————— o ————————

Her eyes were
Dancing,
His eyes were
Prancing,
Until their eyes
Slid into a tango,
The bongo drums
Kept on beating,
Their hearts eating
The old-love crumbs.

This game of pursuit
Is exciting, as it seems
Just like the racehorses,
Who like to run in teams
To reach their destination
Before Ms. Fortune crosses.

If they see encouraging signs
And a sudden spark that shines
In the eyes of their new partners,
They sense success in these augurs
And hang their hopes on this belief,
Then keep dancing with some relief.

ଔ 97 ঞ
Hope

—————————o—————————

Hello, dear
How I fear
You there
I here

Far or near
Don't fear
You'll hear
I'll be there

If you care
Then share
Truth or dare
Be near

Yes, I care
And in fear
Drop a tear
For love is rare

∞ 98 ∞
Cheer Up

—————— ◊ ——————

Cheer up, my darling sweet.
After 5 p.m. have something to eat
And stay away from summer heat.
Also, keep away from a pesky lout
There is nothing left to beat about
In the bush, but only to retreat
To a safe corner in the street;
This I entreat.

Marquez opened our eyes
To life's surprise after surprise,
With his *Hundred Years of Solitude*
And *Of Love and Other Demons*, telling
Of omens, half truths, and half lies,
That come true in the dark dreams
Of restless lives, proving
Nothing dies.

So listen, my darling sweet:
Waves may eat away the shore,
Toss the boat, and break the oar,
Tall mountains may pierce the sky,
Clouds may hide peaks from the eye,
Rivers may dry and sands may melt;
Only *love* is deeply felt and dealt
In life and lore.

Moon's Sister

—————————————— o ——————————————

When the moon saw your proud, uplifted face,
Majestically gazing at the twinkling stars above,
She asked of them, "Is there some other moon
Down there on the earth, attired in silver lace?"

"Oh yes," they replied. "She is a terrestrial damsel,
Graced by gods with a luminous face and form,
Extremely gifted, as you, with wit and charm."
The moon cried, "Then she must be no Jezebel."

"Most certainly not," they chimed, with reason:
"She is gracious of manner, made of your beams,
A happy denizen of the earth, but it also seems
She does change her form with time and season.

"In the mornings she rises as sun from the ocean,
Her hair spread in all directions as rays in motion.
In the evenings, she dances among the tall trees,
Rustling their leaves, arching the sky with ease.

"In the spring, she becomes the lily of the valley,
With sensuous little white flowers, eager to dally.
In the summer, she assumes the form of a peach,
With delicate fuzz and fragrance, ready to teach

"The art and craft of love, like her cousin Venus.
In the fall, she turns into a crisp, rosy-juicy apple.
In the winter she turns into a kitten most supple.
O dear moon, your sister isn't only of one genus."

ཨ 100 ༄

Apsara

———————————— o ————————————

You are far more than I can describe:
Heaven-sent, condensed and centralized
1n a material form a spirit—crystalized,
Difficult to hold, illusive to abstract.

It is easy and uneasy to fall in love with you,
For you are both a real and an imagined person
Who is half in heaven and half on this earth,
Bound to morals and also to wanton mirth.

This combination of your traits and nature
Is most fascinating but also most curtailing
Of the inner freedom that one seeks in love.
So, my angel, how can I find my repose now?

It is easier to think of you rather than to court
An Apsara from the heaven's overarching Court.
Yet I would be most delighted to see you again,
Whenever you descend from the heaven to earth!

≪ 101 ≫
Bottled Perfume

—————————— ◊ ——————————

You are like a bottled perfume
Imprisoned in a smoky vessel of glass,
Both of them exquisitely designed,
But never opened, never aired,
Never held or inhaled or applied;
Yet by all vainly admired.

You live behind a stone wall
Surrounded by a hedge too tall
Whose roots have strangled
The cable that feeds your telephone—
Sitting alone mutely on a table
Waiting for it to ring.

It is now time for you to wake up
And sing to the blue bells ringing,
And hear birds singing their songs.
So instead of remaining behind
The locked doors hiding your charm,
Come out on your vined balcony
And spread your persona and perfume.

Ꮺ 102 ᏕᏅ
Misplaced Love

———————— o ————————

I threw it all away
that seemed to be mine—
pen and paper and computer,
and swirling thoughts in mind—
by which, I had fancied,
I could find me
peace, place, and fame immediately.

Thus bereft of the medium
I knew reasonably well,
I sought refuge in my tongue
to tell you this side of my story:
Oh! how I lost my wings
and how fast I fell
from heaven to hell.

I was once living
with a lovely lady,
but the time I spent on my computer
—writing and rewriting my lines—
robbed her of my passionate company.
So while I was composing love poems,
she was getting closer to my neighbor.

On finding this,
I was terribly distraught
and pleaded with her to forgive me;
instead, she kicked me out of her life quickly.
It was like a soaring eagle
struck by hail and caught;
even, a roaring lion
silenced by a shot.

೦ 103 ೦
Seeking Atonement

———————————— o ————————————

Talking with you this morning
Was like walking on thin ice,
Which comes with its own price:
Each step sounding a warning!

Your recently listed accusations
May be either true or false,
But are these not clear calls
Of anguish that can't be scoffed?

My Love, you feel most injured,
Lied to, and cleverly fooled,
Unjustly caught and spooled;
But these feelings are conjured.

Yet I can't ignore how you feel;
Therefore, I must quickly own
My responsibility and atone:
Kneel and pray for you to heal.

If you think my love is a big lie,
Then I have failed to show it,
Or you have seen in me a foe;
These silly imaginings must go.

They don't do justice to reason
Or to our feelings for each other,
But reflect our ruffled emotions
That can't be called treason.

Believe it or not, I'm concerned
About your emotional state
And wrestle daily against hate
Not to let it embitter our fate.

∝ 104 ∞
Your Sorrow

―――――――――――― o ――――――――――――

Your sorrow surpasses mine
More than you allow me to see;
Yet its quickly fading shadow
Is clearly visible to me.

I too am sorrowing for you,
With love—unbounded and free;
But my sorrows, in your absence,
Find no expression to relieve me.

You and I occupy the same space,
But we measure time differently;
You see the *past* in your *future*,
Forgetting the *present* intently.

The difference between you and me
Is not as large as it seems to be.
You take the *present* for granted;
I see it as a haven for you and me.

Stop raking the ashes of past history.
Stop aching for the future mystery.
We can't bend the time's two ends,
So let's enjoy what the *present* lends.

This world is not a stifling place
Deserving our dismay or derision,
But our thankfulness, for the solace
That *time* provides without omission.

Time is not a river that flows by
Under our wakeful or sleeping eye;
It is a rainbow of feelings in space,
Carrying us along in its embrace.

So why should we grieve or sorrow
For the past errors or the future fears
When *today* our hearts are still beating
And the gifts of love and life greeting?

❧ 105 ❧
Desperation

———————————— o ————————————

Tick-tock, tick-tock went the willful clock.
Testy thoughts streamed in a flock
And kept me awake until the dawn,
When black dew settled on the lawn.

Clop, clop pounded my tired heart.
Every irregular beat gave me a start.
The night grew darker and very long;
I couldn't even hum a rag of a song.

Click, click, you go shod in the green
Sandals, hugging your planter's arch.
With uplifted heals you boldly march
Over the cast glances, gallant or mean.

Oh! your graceful steps waste no time.
They perform a dance in perfect rhyme
To the admiring eyes and choked sighs
From those who give you new highs.

Darling! it is now very hard to hide.
There is no way out but for us to abide
By our human nature, so we may find
What goes on in your heart and my mind!

☙ 106 ❧
My Dear

─────── o ───────

When you tell me,
"I *was* yours,"
Or
"You *had* me,"
My head aches,
My heart breaks.

What is the sense
In using *past tense?*
When the fact is
I *am* yours forever
And have you always
In my heart, I swear.

The *present tense*
In my heart's speech,
I pray, should reach
Your faltering sense
That I am still hoping
To be with you hence.

But if you have given
Me up for some other
To seek some solace,
I'll tell my heart to hush
And beg you not to blush
For having said, seriously,
"I will always love you."

ca 107 so
Desire

———— o ————

If
you're still
on his hook,
then let him reel
you ashore, sans grief,
you'll breathe once again
through your palpating gills
to your cardio-vesicular relief;
and shun your fear and disbelief.

But!
if you're the one
angling,
and he slipped
off the tangled line,
then try again and again,
for you've so much to gain
from swiftly landing him flat
on your luscious, mossy bank.

Yet!
one way or other,
even better,
it will fill the cup
of your pent-up desire,
for the sensations honed,
but long enough postponed,
that fevered your brain a lot
and broke my craving heart.

○ 108 ○
Make a Choice

———————— o ————————

How can I doubt
When you say,
"No, I have not."
For don't we know
That you simply can't,
For the darned reason
That you may be caught,
And so ought.

Some like it hot,
But you like it warm;
In superficial pleasures
You find peculiar charm.
As butterflies to flowers
Do adoringly advance,
To imagined lovers,
You tap dance.

Just try to distinguish
Red flame from the blue:
First is easy to extinguish;
Second heats you so true.
So make your choice
On the color blue;
Its intensity
Comes through.

You ain't no fool,
With looks so cool,
When we fully know
You don't mindlessly sow

Shriveled seeds of discontent
In hearts solely intent
On loving you,
Only you.

౧ 109 ౸
Don't Deny the Truth
———————————— o ————————————

You would do what you said you wouldn't,
Of this I had no doubt from the beginning.
The promise you made in this case couldn't
Be true, for a new love is always beckoning.

I didn't ask, require, or even expect of you
To give up your incessant longing for love,
Sought in pursuit of fame and of variety too.
So why wouldn't you take a new lover now?

You liked to be held from spring to winter,
Cuddled, kissed, rolled up and then down.
How can you now from these joys splinter
And not let down, for the other, your gown.

You and I used to climb walls to make love.
We wouldn't lie still till our lights went out.
The old lover gone, look for a new one now;
You will, otherwise, lose your sexual clout.

So cling to your new love on the featherbed,
And hold him snugly in your tropical groves,
Whispering words that can't be openly said
But swell the torrid waves crashing in droves.

Don't deny the truth its due place in your life.
You deserve to be worshiped by gods, not men.
Get your druthers and try—be some god's wife.
You'll be free to glide, and freer to slide, then.

❧ 110 ❧
Tears

―――――――――――――――― ○ ――――――――――――――――

Tears—shed for shame or sorrow,
Or of pain from a crushing blow,
Or for a promised joy tomorrow
Look alike, but differ in their glow
When seen in the light of feelings,
Which accompany their flow.

Tears of shame have a scarlet hue
Of pain and sorrow—a shade blue.
Yet, all in all, as they slip and fall
From the laden eyes and eyelashes
Down my love's face—in a squall,
My heart sinks and crashes.

When I see the ruby drops swelling
In her sideways-looking, misty eyes,
I promptly join her with my cries.
For the guilt feeling she has, defies
All remedies—medical or otherwise;
For she is a captive to sweet lies.

But if her tears have a bluish touch
And fall like a cascading stream,
I don't know for sure, but this much:
That in her soul some sorrow screams,
Hard to let go, but harder to keep;
Then I offer her my shoulder to weep.

❦ 111 ❧
Deception and Jealousy

———————————— o ————————————

Is this what you wanted all along?
Hush my voice and mute my song!
Erase my memory, held too long!
Push me to where I don't belong!
If so, then whom did you wrong.
Me! I bet you aren't that strong.

Was it fair to have fooled me thus?
When there was no reason to bus
Your charm to all in the omnibus,
Casting lusty eyes without any fuss,
Reaching out like a hungry octopus,
Piling brazen shame on both of us?

Scheming is your trade, O wily one,
Dreaming of others is your only fun,
Preferring the married—well done—
Equipped with a small or a big gun!
(You do quickly understand a pun.)
You are always ready to be undone.

There is a way to save your red face:
Carry it neatly packed in a suitcase.
Drop it quietly at your lover's place,
And let him figure out how to erase
The dark red lies that lace your face
And save you from further disgrace.

❧ 112 ❧
Contention

———————————— ◦ ————————————

You accuse me of cursing you and your clan,
Mercilessly destroying your ego and élan,
While I know how brazenly you kept calling
Me and my friends by names quite appalling.

But is there any truth in words said in anger?
Is there any merit in letting them linger?
Whose victory is there in fighting forever?
Whose defeat is there in condoning never?

Over and over we repeat the same old line,
Like a broken record that was once fine;
But now the time to discard it has come,
Our injured pride mustn't make us dumb.

What purpose is there in holding a grudge?
What point is there in never ever to budge?
What honesty is there in not being fair?
What beauty is there when no one is dear?

You turn some simple words on their head,
Drawing meanings never intended or said.
Your hurt feelings bring up long-gone issues,
Then your eyes hide behind tears and tissues.

I was then, as now, seeking a life with you,
Of love and peace, with complications few,
Which are easy to handle, but not the kind
That leave you drained and perplexed to find.

ೞ 113 ൞
Metamorphosis

——————————— o ———————————

I find I am changing little by little each day.
Metamorphosis of some kind! You may say,
Of the mind more than my body, by the way.

Be not beguiled. I look the same as yesterday,
Yet I recognize myself less and less each day;
A cursed knife has cleft me in a strange way.

She was like a mirror to my mind and soul;
One look from her eyes made me whole.
Oh, I placed all my hopes in a crystal bowl.

She was quite lovely, loving, kind, and just,
But battered by a mindless war—if you must
Know the truth—turning a diamond into dust.

For she was torn by savage notions of love,
Placing love of love and freedom far above;
This tossed her from man to man anyhow.

Her wandering spirit could not distinguish
How her lovers would be driven to anguish
If she couldn't her inane desires extinguish.

Whenever she set her heart on just any one,
Her love dance began with the morning sun
In stringed overtures until the prize was won.

Flirtation would start with a genial discourse,
With colleagues, clients, and guests, of course,
Provoking a romantic interest with silent force.

She knew how to make them depend on her.
Using her charm and office, she made them
Settle cases on terms she alone could offer.

I watched her clever pattern from the tower
And confronted her delicately in our bower,
But my protestations had no effect or power.

I couldn't stop her from her destructive ways,
Thus I hated and loved her on alternate days,
And this process pushed my mind into a haze.

The creeping weeds in my brain I couldn't trim.
Doubt filled my reckoning vessel to the brim.
My heart grew sore, my mind wretchedly grim.

With my grief growing day by day, a big change
Came over me—a change frighteningly strange,
In that my mind wandered over a bizarre range.

The solid rock I stood on went soft and spongy.
The rose bushes in the backyard turned mangy.
My reason went up and down like on a bungee.

I combed the murky waters of stagnant pools,
Flew into the dark clouds tethered to spools
Of horrid ideas that swirl in the heads of fools.

But nowhere did I find a single crumb of truth
That would guide me home as it did poor Ruth,
So I remained trapped in my own foggy booth.

Now, as I am trying to crawl out of my space,
I sense my mind is broken and bound in a case
Similar in substance to a beetle's body and face.

The end of my transformation isn't easy to tell.
My incoherent thoughts can't escape my shell,
But I am trying best to break free from this hell.

⊘ 114 ⊘
Love's Refrain

<hr>

Why have I placed my happiness
In your hands
And kept my hopes in the haziness
Of arid lands?

Why do I crave for summer breeze
In winter freeze,
Search for green in the sapless trees
That do not please?

Why do I wait for the sun to shine
On the cloudy days,
When it is the rain that is just fine
In so many ways?

Why do I thirst for a word from you,
Who is always busy
With tight schedules of multiple hue
That make me dizzy?

Why not place my heart elsewhere
To provide it some rest?
Why not quench it in a pool of fire
Where life is toasted best?

Why not!

෨ 115 ෨
Love's Demise

———————————— o ————————————

Alas, we have reached an impasse!
You by your reckoning and reason,
I by mine; neither willing to unmask
Self-deception and pride in the season
Of fall, when the apples ripen and ask
The arch serpent its poison to pass.

Yes, we have caused hurt and pain
To each other, but it is hard to grasp:
Why we can't break free and rise again
From the cave of shadows to vivid light,
Where eagles soar high without a gasp,
And larks their wings and songs regain!

But is it now possible to easily resume
The same old exciting song and to presume
That our Eden's gate is not too far away,
But lies within easy reach of love's way?
Somehow our destiny's map has changed,
Its colors and contours artfully rearranged.

So here we are now—witlessly reaping
The bitter fruit of betrayal, and weeping
To wash our minds clean of life's deceit,
Yet unwilling to confess or admit defeat,
Out of fear, self-preservation, or conceit.

When truth dies, love can't be speaking.

❧ 116 ❧
Bitten by Light

―――――――――― 0 ――――――――――

I tend to see a light
Where there's none,
So little for heart's delight,
So much for reality shun.

You had trained me to believe
Every word you casually said,
But the cards in your sleeve,
I found, were with faces red.

How can I read between the lines
When the writing is overwritten
And the red ink starkly shines
Its light on a heart sorely bitten?

❧ 117 ❧
Differences

─────────── ० ───────────

Why do you like me?
I am not your kind,
I am not that kind.
You like leisure and love,
With all their passing flavors;
I salute life—the arching bow,
Stringing it with mundane labors,
Wetted in boiling blood of love.

Why do you want me?
When you know it:
Candles can't be lit
On the stormy shores of doom,
Which beckon me to face soon
Myriad fears that quietly bloom,
Even after the passing of a typhoon.
Why do you crave the waning moon?

I may seem more than one,
Combining images of them all,
Like a broken mirror reflecting the sun;
It's my scattered fragments you recall.
But I am overlain by earth and snow,
Composting with the fallen leaves,
Yet you imagine or pretend to know
That I am hiding under your eaves.

You are like lightning,
Streaking the night in a flash,
A bright corolla quickly opening,
Pouring out its streams of scent

To drown the unsuspecting traveler
In the sweet opiates of dreams,
Lodged in the sleepy eyes of the reveler
That wake him by his own silent screams.

You are like no one I have seen:
Loving, but combing the dark streets
With a thirsty tongue and senses keen,
Licking salty popsicles for sweet treats,
Gulping down adorations and moans
In rocking cars and on telephones.
I can't blind my eyes or plug my ears,
Or wash my wounds in acid tears.

I loved you once to distraction;
Wide and deep was my attraction.
My prayers kept the stars gazing,
But all this madness was amazing.
Then I heard the snakes by my feet hissing,
While we were bloodying our lips kissing;
I felt an invisible finger jab at my chest,
And a voice in my heart said the rest.

༺ 118 ༻
Let Her Go

---o---

She has decided to go.
That much I know,
For water must flow
Or else icicles grow.

Yet I mutely wonder:
Why this silly blunder?
Is it resident in their gender?
Why no light, but only thunder!

Neither fine mist nor rain
In the eyes seemingly in pain
Give any pause to entertain
A doubt or refrain.

A smile on their face
Is often hard to trace
To its meaning or case,
Crocheted in delicate lace.

Should I stop or let her go?
Give a chance for a miracle to show!
No, my heart, you better learn to grow
Peaceful, and let her wonder to and fro.

෬ 119 ෨
Goodbye

—————————— ○ ——————————

I lie awake
All night a lot,
In my cold bed burning hot,
Asking, why did you cut the tie
Without saying a goodbye.

We were like
Two billing doves,
Two wings of a bird,
Two peas in a pod;
That is why it is so damn hard.

It's vain to feign
That "I am not deeply hurt,"
Or "I don't care anymore,"
Or even "This too shall pass."
I wish I could say it, but I can't, alas.

For that isn't how I feel,
And I suppose, neither do you.
But it's true: you broke the deal,
So how can I simply repeal
A bitter fact with a feel-good lie.

So let me see
From your point of view
And imagine what you would say:
"I didn't want to leave,
But you gave me no sign to believe."

In my innocence,
Which was of essence
To our coexistence,
I kept hoping we to each other belonged;
But your roving eyes proved me wrong.

So why don't I
Get a shard of sleep in my eye?
But keep on tossing and turning
In my cold bed, burning hot,
When there are better things to sort.

↷ 120 ↶
Search Your Heart
—————————————— o ——————————————

Touch your heart and you will see
Clearly in your mind's discerning eye
That you've judged me differently
Since we exchanged a goodbye.

Until then, I was the only one
Whose company you wouldn't shun,
For then we had a life you so craved,
And every danger you so gladly braved.

Now you avoid me, as if I am a pain
In your eye that can't open or shut.
Is it because we have together lain,
And now you with another cohabit?

I don't hold this a bit against you,
For everyone does the same shit;
But you were among those few
Who proclaim they don't fall in it.

If your conscience is hurting you,
Where did you get it all at once?
Or is it the fear of your new beau,
That he too may call you a dunce.

My dear, you don't have to change
Your old tactics to please your beau.
It'll make you stranger than strange
And pull down your cover and show.

So please don't judge me differently,
Or your own self—for it is what it is:
Human beings tied to desires endlessly
Search for new pleasures constantly.

❧ 121 ❧
Poor Return

———————————————— o ————————————————

You gave me joy; I gave you sorrow,
With vague promises of tomorrow,
Prolonging them both endlessly.

You gave me love; I gave you tears,
Which submerged me in a sea of fears
And unnecessary cares—senselessly.

You gave me hope and reason to live;
I squandered it all in moments so few,
Like water running out of a rusty sieve.

You tried to spread happiness over all;
But I was bound by my history to fall
On the thorns of life, poisoned by gall.

You saw beauty in perfect harmony;
I remained captive to useless duty,
Drowning myself in mere absurdity.

Why were we so poorly fashioned?
Why were we so foolishly frightened?
Why were we so damn easily broken?

If we had eschewed our human frailty
And carefully measured our reality,
Our dreams would have come true.

Life's sorrows may seem to have no end,
For they greet you at each bloody bend,
But we shouldn't give up our hope easily.

ᖇ 122 ᖃ
Undoing

———————— o ————————

Those pretty wrongs that liberty commits,
When I am absent from thy heart.
—William Shakespeare, "Sonnet 41"

———————— o ————————

If I could see you once again!
Not where we had met or been before:
The first time, when we fell in love,
Or the last, where we missed our shore,
Or where the demons of desire roam;
But there where the air is crisp
And kissed by love's mist.

There, witnessed by a clear stream,
Flowing over the bedrocks of my dream,
Through a meadow where buttercups are ready
To fill our cups with honeyed cream;
I would open my heart to open your eyes.

Near that glistening stream of pure reason,
In the sweetly flowering season of thought,
I could, my love, easily unguise the treason
That sundered our bonded souls apart,
Just like a hammer breaking a rock.

Alas! it was only our ego's doing,
Seeking wantonly a way out from losing
Our false sense of freedom, liberally oozing
In all directions, out of an endless craving
For attention that became our undoing.

Ask, "Can freedom-seeking undo love?"
Yes, if we confuse freedom with liberty
And keep stretching the latter too far
Without giving a thought or pause;
Then such liberty becomes the cause.

There is now enough reason to uncause
Our senselessly tragic undoing, because
Life without you isn't worth a dime,
So let us rejoin in one perfect rhyme
The scattered words of our poem.

↪ 123 ↩
I Remember

———————— ○ ————————

I remember, I remember
Your each gold-minted word
Uttered just once,
But twice heard.
First, when it hit my resonating drum,
Leaving me momentarily numb,
Then when it reached my heart
And woke me up with a start.

I remember, I remember,
What you quietly said,
Jumping off the bed,
On that glorious morn of May:
*"I love you so,
Please don't go."*
I couldn't believe my ears or heart
Or heed this wondrous thought.

The seed of sorrow thus sown,
Quickly grew into a rank weed
Nourished by tears of resentment,
Mistrust, and badly bruised sentiment!
Puzzling as it may seem,
Our love was like a wild dream,
Indeed, a torrent that cried aloud
For truth—hiding in a dark cloud.

I distinctly remember
How sorrowfully we said our adieus,
Assuring each other of exchanging news.
But the lamps of love in our eyes

Could not be dimmed by our cries
Of despair that fogged the chamber,
Still shining your amber eyes,
Which I will always remember.

The memory of our painful parting
Will remain in my soul till its departing.

❧ 124 ❦
Star Light

──────────── o ────────────

When I lie under the canopy of night
It isn't to read or count the stars
But to invite their fading light
Into my heart that chars
Ready to extinguish and crash
Like a last dying ember on its ash

Oh, let that Delphian dream come
And hold me in its hypnotic trance
Easing my tearing tension some
With a heartwarming glance
From your emerald eyes
To sleep without sighs

I miss you very much
Your smell and touch
Far away from my reach
These memories can't beseech
You to be generous with your dole
Though they are imbued in my very soul

❁ 125 ❁
Express Letter

————————— o —————————

Yes, I am still crazy about you
Even after our byes
Uttered in sighs
Tears in eyes
And cries
So long ago and after so many tries
To resurrect our love and lives

I still miss you day and night
Holding in my heart
Your loving heart
Only to smart
With art
That keeps me thinking a lot
What I sought and what I got

How can I deny what was true
Then—even as now
Adoring you so
O angel blue
It is true
I find it hard to live without you
For persons like you are but few

I can't resurrect my happiness
In such a loneliness
Much sadness
It's madness
I confess
So I'm sending this letter express
But need to find your new address

ೲ 126 හ
Dreams

———— 0 ————

You come and go
In my dreams as you please.
Is it just to show
How you can tease?

What do you find
In being so unkind
To a man sleeping blind,
Yanking him out of his mind?

Last night, in my sleep,
I saw you by my side asleep;
My heart took a joyous leap,
Alas! this dream I couldn't keep.

I opened my eye,
But you weren't there;
Your stealthy flight all senses defy,
Waking up only an unknown fear.

Bare feet you roam in
All the corridors of my mind,
Like a Hindu quietly uttering Aum,
Appealing to a deity to be very kind.

I am under no illusion
That your visitations speak of love;
You want to keep me in that delusion
Until you purge me out of your mind.

∝ 127 ∾
Troubling Absence

O devouring Sleep!
You come to life
Only in my dreams,
When my neurons are set to fire
By the choked desire
Held back in my sleepless state.

Then you resurrect from dust
And howl like a starving beast
Chained to the fixed wheel
Of revolving despair,
On finding she isn't there
Now not anymore.

My dreams are serpentine;
They have no sense of time.
Sinuously they come and go
Like a stream that doesn't flow
But falls into a deep abyss
Of misery and sorrow.

I used to sleep untroubled
When she was there with me:
In the same bed—cuddled
To the free protons of my being—
With her fiery red locks
Spread on my burning chest.

Now that she has gone
With the searing desert wind
To a distant green oasis,
My sleep has sunk into dreams
Of spectral nature, I confess:
Sand dunes, snakes, and sadness.

ଔ 128 ଓ
Peace Comes Gently

───────── o ─────────

"Hope it's a lovely day,"
She said,
Waking up from her bed,
Slowly inhaling the fragrant breeze
Coming from a stand of sweet peas
In the backyard—blooming gay
On this beautiful day.

She put on a silk gown
And stepped down
To her redwood deck,
Enclosed by a black-painted iron guard,
Overlooking the garden in the backyard,
Where the sweet peas and roses in bloom
Were beaming to dispel her gloom.

She looked at the flowers
Wistfully, recalling
How he had planted them,
The rootstocks and seeds on his knees,
After she and he had become pledged lovers
And given each other the keys to unlock
Their desires and mysteries.

But now he wasn't there
To hold her close or near;
They had separated out of fear
Of each other's cheating tendency
That poisoned their trust and intimacy.
They seemed to have done nothing wrong,
Yet suspicion rooted and grew strong.

The separation was hard to bear,
For their love was not an ordinary affair.
They had dared and sacrificed too much,
So they suffered in silence day and night.
The freedom they'd sought became a fright,
Like an albatross round the neck,
Bringing fear and gloom.

Gone from her world
Was the thrill and comfort of his love
(The wind under the wings of the dove);
And he too was mercilessly hurled
On a thorny ground with his hands bound;
But both buried their heads in the sand
And ate the dust of their love by hand.

As she looked at the flowers below,
Trying hard to soak in their glow,
In her broken heart, beating slow,
She felt his spirit magically flow
From the garden into her whole frame
(Body and mind and soul—all together)
Bringing her peace, whispering her name.

෬ 129 ෨
The Passion to Keep

―――――――― o ――――――――

I must my petty passions set aside:
Forget the roses blooming in my yard,
Where I spend my whole day to hide
From myself, my neighbor, and God;
Surely, I must this passion set aside.

As for the books that burn my eyes
Through the long hours past midnight,
When these romances I try to fantasize,
Just, by proxy, to draw a little delight;
Surely, I must this passion set aside.

On the wet rainy days, I like watching
Raindrops beating time on the leaves,
Making their dance quite eye-catching.
Watching this, my heart gently heaves,
But I must this passion too set aside.

These silly passions of mine helped me
Hasten the flow of days and nights,
So I could sooner my real passion see,
Unfolding in all her dazzling lights,
Like a well-lit harbor nestled in a lee.

Now I have received this intimation
That she is coming back to live with me
In my lonely aboard, which is needed
Not only for her to take the reins again
But to undo the guilt of forsaking me.

She has been my only love and passion,
Consuming every drop of attention,
Radiating essence, as a cashmere rose.

From her mind, loving visions arise
To her voluptuous lips that surprise
And transport you to a heavenly isle,
Where the sun plays hide and seek
Through the moving clouds—to peek
At her sinuous form and emerald eyes,
Reaching out for passionate highs.

This is the only passion I want to keep.

෴ 130 ෴
Do the Dead Talk?

――――――――――――――― o ―――――――――――――――

It is often said, the dead don't talk.
They smolder under earth and rock
Or go down the river in burnt ash
And vanish after a brief splash.
But I wonder if it's completely true.
And do the dead also hold this view?

No, it can't be even partially correct,
For we know some do fully resurrect.
And I have heard myself the dead speak
From wherever they be, if we avidly seek
The memories—of those we truly loved,
Held in the faded threads of our shroud.

Some of the dead let their persona heave
Through a rich legacy of deeds they leave
In science, philosophy, commerce, or art.
But I am not pursuing this line of thought.
Here I am speaking of the sensory fare
That the dead offer to the unaided ear.

In the winter of my soul, when I clean
The ash-filled fireplace to light, I just lean
To hear the quaint swishing sound of air,
Bringing the many whisperings of my dear
Departed love distinctly to my thirsty ear,
And her lovely voice I do once again hear.

A number of intimate letters quietly rest
In a locked compartment of my old chest.
When I open them again and begin to read,

I hear her voice flow with each line, indeed,
Intoning each word in its expressed feeling
That I may have missed in my first reading.

In the spring season, I see her on the deck,
Watching me pruning the roses and plucking
The older ones whose color time has faded.
I hear her calling me in a voice too jaded,
Admonishing not to cut the fading flower,
For it has still a life left to charm its lover.

෬ 131 ෭
A Vision

———————————— ○ ————————————

What fortitude the soul contains,
That it can so endure
The accent of a coming foot,
The opening of a door!
—Emily Dickinson

———————————— ○ ————————————

What should I do!
When I hear once again,
after the stream has dried up,
leaving a trickle of memories,
the familiar sound of her feet,
muffled by the soft slippers,
smelling of bruised roses,
outside my door?

Yes, we're once together,
sweetly killing each other
with the insanity of love;
but she's no more now,
and I live with my fate
in the womb of pain,
waiting to see her
face-to-face again.

So what should I do
when I don't know
if I am awake or in a dream
seeming to sense her close by?

Just stop breathing to hear well
or inhale the perfumed air to tell
if she is really there, still hesitating
to own me again—with a kiss to kill!

I'm too confused but refuse to believe
that she doesn't want my pain to relieve;
So I jump from my bed and rush to the door.
As I open it, she imperially steps onto my floor.

৹ 132 ৹
Love beyond Death

————————————— ○ —————————————

My thirst has congealed
On my lips—a stone I see;
I fell in your river and healed,
But came out still thirsty!

The arrows from your eyes
Pierced my heart's sanctuary,
Lifting my soul to the skies,
Blown by your cute archery.

So many have admired you,
But they all remained alive
And fully able to continue
Striving for the honey hive.

Now, since you have killed me,
I am entombed in darkness,
Begging death to let me see
You again—my claim to press.

As moths love to see a flame,
Wherein they burn and die,
My love for you is no game,
As death and I together lie.

❧ 133 ❧
Your Silence

—————— o ——————

The day has folded,
The church bells chime,
You haven't spoken
For a long time.

The snow has melted,
Bare ground meets the eye,
Your prolonged silence
Makes me cry.

The daffodils are swaying
In the spring breeze,
My heavy heart is still
In the deep freeze.

Why do you hold me
In your invisible arms,
When you are distantly
Withholding your charms?

A moonless night
Is now upon me;
Sleepless, lonely I will be,
Unable to touch you or see.

This world will go on,
No matter what we do.
My life has shortened
For want of you.

☙ 134 ❧
Love's Labor Lost

———o———

There is a vaselike jar
On my kitchen shelf,
Full of sweet-scented honey
Stolen from a hive of busy bees.
They had built it in my backyard.

The jar reminds me
Of my bygone honey—
With slim waist and syrupy eyes,
Quiet, funny, and very sunny—
In love, till we broke apart.

Like me, the bees are
In turmoil, quite aghast
At their love's labor lost;
Buzzing angrily, they are now
Vainly looking for the cause.

Loss of labor, money, or honey
To creatures—big or small—
Causes injury that's visible to all,
Except the Wall Street climbers,
Whose fortunes rise and fall.

C𝖱 135 𝖘𝖔
Guilty Conscience
———————————— o ————————————

My laden thoughts have plunged me
Into a hazy stream of consciousness,
Now trying hard to discern and see:
Why in my dream a bottomless abyss
Appeared so suddenly in front of me.

I was dreaming but seemingly awake:
Walking alone on the shore of a lake
Where I saw two familiar figures ahead
—A woman and a child, attired in red—
Shrouded in the wafting plumes of mist,
Standing dejectedly under a willow tree
Uttering mournful cries intermittently.

Thinking they may need some help
I hastened towards them hurriedly,
But on reaching the grim location
Found no trace of them under the tree—
Only its dropping branches swaying eerily.

Puzzled, I turned my head towards the lake
And saw a small white boat being paddled
By the woman in red without a break
Trying to reach the opposite shore
As quickly as it was possible to make.
The child was sitting behind her rigidly,
Looking at the frantic oars intently.

The woman was bending and pulling
But the boat was making no progress
As if it were anchored or unwilling

To move forward with any eagerness.
Sensing doom, I was gripped by panic.

Since the boat was far out in the lake
And I didn't know how to swim across,
I began shouting for their safety's sake,
But they didn't respond to my frantic calls.

Soon a monstrous sound came from the lake,
Its surface had frozen into a sheet of ice
That cracked and crumbled in a trice
Sending shock waves through my spine.

There was no trace of the white boat,
Nor of the two persons attired in red,
Nor of the placid waters of the lake,
But only a frightening black abyss
In front of my two unbelieving eyes
Which were wide awake in my dream—
The horrid dream that made me scream.

Trembling all over, I managed to get up
From my bed, its sheets soggy with sweat.
I held my head in my hands to concentrate
And it came to me slowly: the woman and
The child in red were no other but my own
Family! whom I had abandoned to infamy.

❧ 136 ❧
Shadow of Memories

Under the shadow of my memories,
I bask, lounge, doze, and fall asleep,
Entering a dream world of ecstasies,
Where, fully awakened, I then keep
Flipping the pages of my history,
Some still legible in black and white,
Others faded into grays of mystery,
But, all combined, beguiling insight.

Yet no page so vital or to this equal,
For it keeps me wondering why
My eye fell on that priceless jewel,
Which, on credit, I couldn't buy,
And lacking courage, couldn't steal.
This jewel was no other but her love,
Which I coveted and wanted to seal,
But to devil and death, lost the deal.

℘ 137 ℘
Ode to the Heart
——————————————— o ———————————————

Thanks to the human heart by which we live,
Thanks to its tenderness, its joys, and fears,
To me the meanest flower that blows can give
Thoughts that do often lie too deep for tears."
—William Wordsworth, "Ode: Intimations of
Immortality from Recollections of Early Childhood"
——————————————— o ———————————————

O my heart! guide me with discerning light.
Lead my mind to find what is true and right
As I look far and see the *word* in my soul,
To write simply in praise of *you* as my goal.

The land where the ancestors live and die,
Where civilizations flourish or in ruins lie,
There the human heart is a sacred ground
To mankind's ventures and victories found.

In the heart lies the garden of life and love,
The ground of intuition and know-how,
Where questions of being—who and how—
Are churned to find peace here and now.

The lands where hopes are sown to grow
And our fears weeded out—clearly show
How hate turns into love by a just reflection
Of light that hearts hold in contemplation.

Whereas the mind seems to know it all,
Its ability to sense being in no way small.
But trapped in the dented wheels of logic,
The mind is subservient to heart's magic.

The wondrous magic the heart supplies,
The rhyme and rhythm it quietly applies
To every part of the body and mind,
Gives us a vision of the unity in mankind.

In the lush garden of the heart, flowers don't die,
Leaves don't wither, and love sees eye to eye
With all, and anon, drawing close in unity
The scattered subjects and ideals of humanity.

In the heart where the soul quietly dwells,
Watching every move and mood that swells
Like a tide in the ocean, bidding one to act:
In a clear-honest-bold manner to resurrect.

The hopes that lie dormant in the mind
When nourished by heart's blood do find
A new strength to resurface and resurrect
And prompt the man not to give up, but act.

Visions in the mind assemble and dissemble
Like clouds herded by wind duly ensemble.
The beating heart spreads the fire of breath
To energize the body and mind until death.

The mind is abstract, the heart concrete,
Yet throbbing and full of feelings discrete.
The mind is too busy processing and turning.
The heart longs for true love and learning.

The mind dwells in a web of nervous matter,
Pushed and pulled, it can go helter-skelter,
But the good heart dwells in the land of love,
And its rhythms are watched from far above.

Visions of the extraordinary or prophetic kind
May arise from an uncommonly gifted mind,
But their actualization takes a brave heart
That is filled with grace and devotion a lot.

A dashing display of valor in love or war
Reflects quality of the hero's mind by far,
Yet without adequate courage in his heart,
Our hero wouldn't be able to stand or start.

We must fight our demons first in our heart,
Banish hate and fear before they begin to rot
The easily corruptible substance of our mind;
For what the heart can see, mind cannot find.

ೕ 138 ೋ
In Conclusion

———————— 0 ————————

Learning a language
that fills
only half a page
will set you free
from the afflictions
of old age.

A happy child
who knows little
pleases all
compared to an old bombast
whose big words and phrases
get you mixed up and lost.

The language of heart
is a fine art,
those who have it
have it all—
attentive ears, trusting eyes,
clear skies.

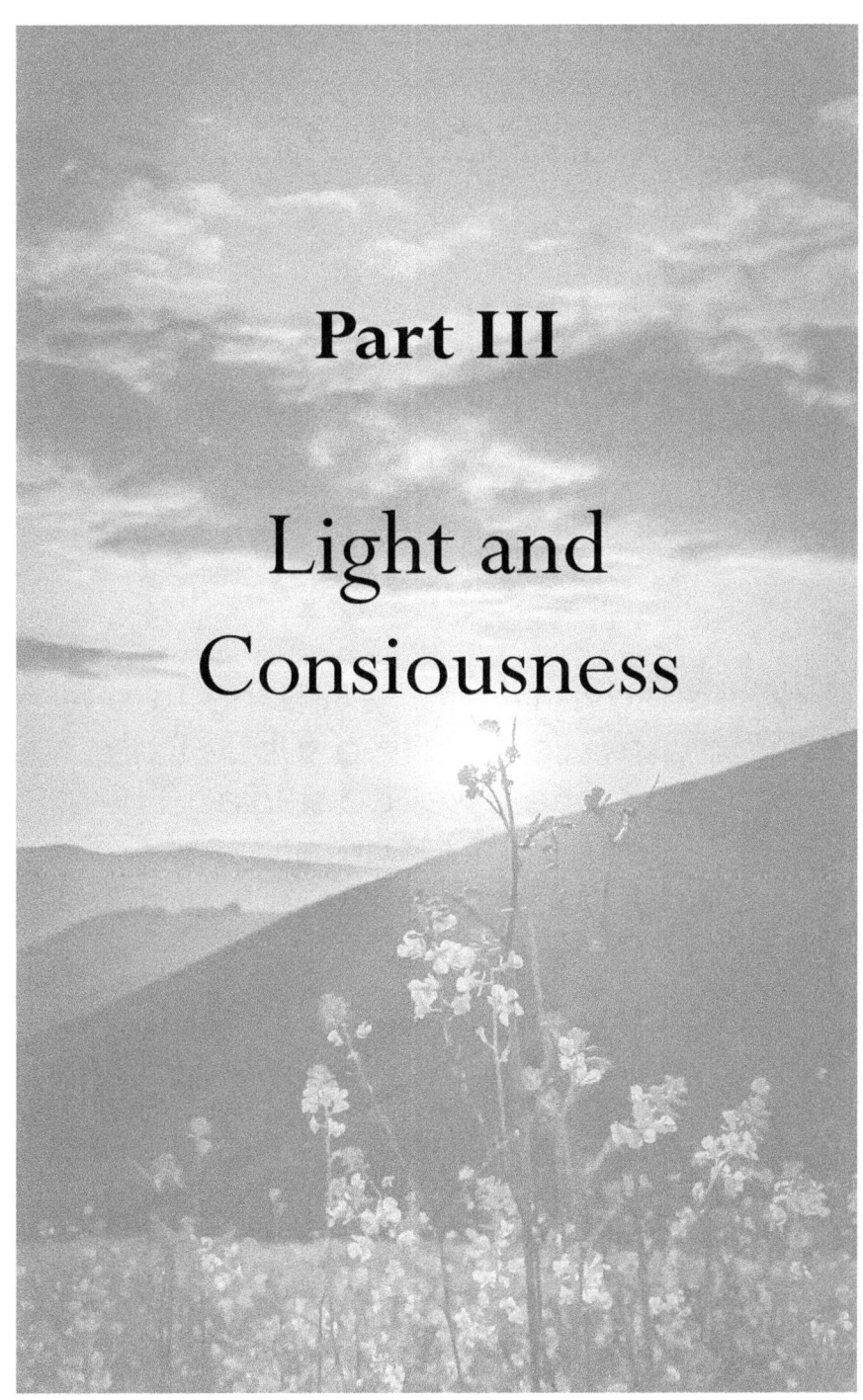

Part III

Light and Consiousness

Light and Consciousness

When He shines, everything
begins to shine.
Everything in this world reflects His light.
—Mundaka Upanishad

In the cave of the Heart, the True I
Radiates alone with a subtle Light
The one essence shining
forth without defect—
Blissful consciousness of Being.
—Oleg Mogilever

Consciousness cannot be accounted
for in physical terms. For consciousness
is absolutely fundamental.
—Ervin Schrödinger

༄ 139 ༅
The Path

———————— o ————————

There
In sorrow
And humility
Lies the secret
Of evolving strength
And unfolding wisdom,
Harnessed by perseverance;
As shown by a wise Nazarene.

This path leads to our freedom
From the grim fetters of desires
That tie us to the yoke of bondage,
Causing us an irreversible damage.

Stuck in the wet, miry furrow, the ox,
With his uplifted eyes, humbly thanks
his Maker
For the downpour that cooled his back,
Giving some respite from his burdens.

Pulling thus the life's drag thru time,
Stop periodically to thank and pray,
So that your fortitude may not flop,
And your resolution doesn't snap.

This process ensures restoration
Of peace in your weary mind,
Stamina in your tired body,
And light in your soul.
As you are restored,
You will achieve
True wisdom
And freedom.

ॐ 140 ॐ
Divine Consciousness

───────── o ─────────

O Thou of whom I am the instrument,
O secret Spirit and Nature housed in me,
Let all my mortal being now be blent
In Thy still glory of divinity.
—Aurobindo Ghose, "Surrender"

───────── o ─────────

O my heart and soul, think of God eternal
In your Self and all around—
Incarnate in:
Seed and flower, in rain and river,
In mind and matter, in thought and speech;
yet so personal, so paternal, so maternal!
That we humans can relate to Him or Her as One;

You are all pervading, all transcending,
All knowing, all sustaining, and All—
Incarnate in:
Each principle and particle of the Universe;
Creating and uncreating from your own Being
All the visible and invisible matter and energy,
Suffusing the Divine Spirit of Consciousness in all.

ᴄ𝕣 141 ᴓ
My Identity

———————— o ————————

I am a part of All there is
—In order or in chaos—
Yet I stand apart from the rest
As an individual, self-aware entity,
Though made of the same stuff
As the earth, the stars, and the cosmic
Dust that together make up the Universe
We can see—barring the dark stuff there be.

So if I am a very tiny part,
How then do I stand apart?

Is it because of the *free will*
With which I am endowed?
Or because of my ego and fear
Of being lumped together with the rest,
Bringing down my status from "the best"?

My mind and consciousness
Tell me otherwise:
"I am wrapped in my identity too much,
Which doesn't allow me to see clearly.
Consciousness is not only localized in the brain,
But spread across the entire Universe.
If it weren't so, how would the Universe grow
From a tiny dot to a humongous size?"

Consciousness is Universe's primary reality
—Call it God's Spirit or Divine Will—
Pervading the Universe and seen as One,
Residing in everything and everyone.

So in this sense, I am a part of and also apart
from that which is the Absolute Truth and Bliss.

ᘓ 142 ᘚ
Character

———————————— o ————————————

O Brilliant Blue Diamond,
What shades of hardness you hide
In your luminous body with pride!
I see you with my mortal eyes
That the whole spectrum can't see,
And there lies my conundrum!—
The light that radiates from you
Comes not only from your margin
But certainly, it has a deeper origin!
You are cut in the shape of a heart
That appears pulsating with life,
Yet, with an edge sharper than a knife,
Leaving no doubt in my mind:
You're a Sapiens of a rare kind.

ॐ 143 ॐ
Light in Sorrow

———— o ————

Pain is a treasure, for it contains mercies;
The kernel is soft when the rind is scrapped off.
—Rumi, "Pain is a Treasure" (translated by F. Hadland Davis)

———— o ————

In sorrow abides the kingdom
Of steadily evolving endurance,
Slowly ripening perseverance,
And gently unfolding wisdom.

But they need sacrifice to mature,
Pain and suffering first to endure,
As the misshapen nugget of gold
Takes heat and hammer to mold.

Ask, "What gain is there in pain
And suffering?" Let me explain:
While pain summons endurance,
So suffering incubates patience.

Pain is a stern teacher of tolerance,
Serving an antidote to arrogance.
On losing a loved one, we sorrow,
Then recover from it tomorrow.

Pain and suffering have a limited span.
They are diffused by time and élan,
By the painfully gained experience
And our wisdom and perseverance.

⤫ 144 ⤬
Somber Thoughts

O! somber thoughts, raise your head
From the murky depths of oceanic floor,
With uplifting power of volcanic force,
And let your clear voice heavenward soar.

You have remained patiently submerged
Under old Neptune's trident for too long,
Lending your words a briny-bitter taste,
And, seemingly, on your lips a sad song.

Grave and melancholy you may seem,
But your ideas do have a sanguine edge.
Colored thus, they do often unsettle us;
But, in truth, to truth you point and pledge.

Dark and drab your appearance may seem
To those who witness you from outside,
But in your thoughts, deep meaning I see,
For they all cant and vagueness kick aside.

A serious purpose they bring to life:
In demanding prudent actions from us,
Somber though they are, so is our strife.
So why shouldn't we our wants confess?

O! somber thoughts, raise your head;
Proclaim the purpose for your existence,
For I know you goad us to move ahead
With courage and wisdom and persistence.

℘ 145 ℘
Chaos and Order

—o—

Everything existing in the universe
is the fruit of chance and necessity.
—Democritus

—o—

As the distant star sheds its bright light
and becomes dim,
As the journeying meteorite in its flight
burns at earth's rim,
As the flowing stream erodes the solid rock
on its own bed,
As the icy wind lifts the swift flying hawk
and lays it dead,
We all are solitary specks of luminous dust
floating in space,
Not so formidable that time's bloodlust
can't easily erase.

So in cosmos lie together *being* and *emptiness*
for some strange reason
Unknown to mortals, but surely evolving
beyond trust or treason.

If that is the order, decree, and destiny
of all there is,
Then what holds us back from an epiphany,
for that too is His?
Why not drink, devour, and conquer *time*
and its tortuous history?
And why not stop *time's* mournful chime,
its unending mystery?

We are told to use *free will* to figure a way out
that would be right;
But none reach the empyrean height without
sacrifice and divine light.

৪৩ 146 ৪৩

Human Folly

———————————— o ————————————

Know then thyself, presume not God to scan,
The proper study of mankind is Man.
Placed on this isthmus of a middle state,
A being darkly wise and rudely great.
—Alexander Pope, "Essay on Man, Epistle II"

———————————— o ————————————

You of myriad woes seem to be seeking
The lightning that sunders the night
And, in a flash, reveals the jagged knife
Buried deep in your soul—illumined by light.

Consumed by endless desires that bred
A being so complex and shrouded in mystery,
You stand forlorn, in utter dread
Of the dark deeds that mark your history.

Oh man! you set yourself above the rest,
To conquer, change, and subdue all,
Hoping to remake nature as suits you best;
But you also let too much to slip and fall.

First of all, your fall from heaven's grace—
Ascribed to your disobedience to God[1]
Or ignorance of your kinship with All[2]—
Has darkly marked your face and race.

———————————

1   The Judeo-Christian view: disobedience to personal God and subsequent fall of Adam
2   The Hindu view: Avidya — lack of knowledge of man's oneness with Brahman
    [Godhead], both views pointing to alienation of man from God.

Was this your sin or God's design?
Or the work of a gift sublime—your ego,
Which was supposed to let you find your way
And assume a rightful place in the divine.

Your trust and perceived relief in *free will*
Is a two-edged sword; it lifts or drowns
Based on thy deeds of good or ill will,
While holding God's *will* to no account!

When left to your own desires and devices,
You chose pride, aggrandizement, and greed;
Filled with lofty thoughts and base vices,
You swayed up and down like a thin reed.

Oh man! now you wonder what went wrong?
Why this war in your soul and the world around?
Why isn't there joyful dance, music, and song?
Why myriad woes remain with you all along?

℘ 147 ℘
Curiosity

———————— ○ ————————

Impelled by my
scientific curiosity,
I took a lovely red rose
clinically apart—
petal by petal,
stamens, ovary, and all—
just to find
the secret of its
fragrance and beauty.

The crimson petals
gathered ruefully
around my restless feet
on the floor—
like splashes of
freshly spilled blood.

Watching the petals
dry out and curl
in the summer heat,
my heart shriveled
and skipped a beat.

I was filled
with shame and sorrow,
thinking what will become of me
if I continue to dissect everything
In pursuit of scientific luminosity;
Instead of simply seeing
truth in beauty!

Then it came to me suddenly, my love:
how I used to show the same curiosity
about your private thoughts and affairs!
It became a stupid cause of our misery.

ೞ 148 ೞ
Thickets and Pickets
———————— o ————————

Walk with me around this last bend;
Our difficult journey is about to end.
We have some more to sense and share:
New ideas and actions to test and dare.

Life's struggles have put us to moping,
But we must keep on searching, hoping
For a divine light to illumine our mind,
To free us from grim fetters of all kind.

Yes, we mope—for want of courage
To clear the dense thickets that encage
Our mortal ideas and actions in a vice.
These thickets bite and blind us in a trice.

We drive stakes and pickets of all kind
In the willing ground of our raw mind,
Then we avidly search around to find
Other ideas or actions that seem to bind

And jive with ours, securely underlined.
This inflates our ego and makes us blind
To opposite ideas that may also hold true
And be similarly impossible to disprove.

So by our own making, picket by picket,
We find ourselves in a blinding thicket
Of ideas and actions that amount to naught,
While we keep on insisting, they ought.

How can we break their pernicious hold?
We ask and ask till we grow very old.
But in our ardent search for a cool spring,
We must first jump through a fiery ring.

We could have taken this path before;
Stars would have led us to the shore.
It would be a much richer, happier time,
With innocence reigning, and no crime.

In our search for truth or beauty, we must
Seek harmony, not by racking logic's dust
To win a point by only its scientific force,
But by an intuitive feel for its fluid course.

So, my loving heart, walk with me
With courage and guiding reason,
That I may not ever forget to see
The truth and beauty in each season.

ᘓ 149 ᘔ
Time

―――――― o ――――――

Devouring Time, blunt thou the lion's paws,
And make the earth devour her own sweet brood,
Pluck the keen teeth from the fierce tiger's jaws,
And burn the long-lived phoenix in her blood.
—William Shakespeare, "Sonnet XIX"

―――――― o ――――――

Time! you swift steed of blinding light,
Straight and sharp as Apollo's arrow bright,
You fly forth without any hindsight or rest,
Piercing cosmic dust and the human breast.

No one can see you fly by, or catch or hold.
You skip quickly by seconds that can't be told.
You leap by eons in steps immeasurably bold
And watch the world in glances divinely cold.

You think you are quite uniform in your stride;
In your measured steps you take immense pride.
But see: a lover finds an hour too short and shy;
The ailing child finds it too long to sleep or cry.

You cast strange spells that are too hard to tell.
You are famed to heal sorrow, yet you compel
The bereaved to stand up and swallow his grief.
You tease and torture, then restore us—in brief.

Time! are you truly the web and warp of space?
Its intangible dimension, its divine cord or lace?
Be whatever thou art, but as I listen to my heart,
Without my *being* you wouldn't stir, nor start.

𝄔 150 ଞ
Is *Time* Real?

---------- ◊ ----------

I sought thee in the timeless halls of space
I sought thee in the spaceless halls of time
But found that time and space do not exist.
—Robert Goslin, "Brahman"

---------- ◊ ----------

When I see *Time* crawling like a snail
And, at times, slithering like a snake,
I don't trust its reality or guise,
Nor do I find in its tricks any surprise.
No doubt, *Time* is a dimension of varying size:
Unmeasurable by our natural or aided eyes.

I think *Time* is a phantom river
Whose source is in our head or mind.
And, therefore, its presence everywhere;
For wherever we go, we take our minds along.
We divide time into past, present, and future
But it's the *Present* that always exists in nature.

Perhaps, past and future lie together as one,
As a big illusion when all is said and done.
I believe it is our and nature's activities
That give us a false feeling about time's flow:
It is the sequence of events that make it so.
Time has no independent being of its own.

So let us not count our lives
In days or years, but by the actions
We take: The things we see and feel,
The way we speak and deal with others,
The joy and enthusiasm we spread in life,
And by respecting each other, our sustaining
Earth, our life-giving Sun, and the Maker of All.

ಚಿ 151 ೞಿ
Origin and Purpose of Time

———————— ◊ ————————

Roll on, you invincible Time…
Weave your way through space,
Creating a seamless fabric
That holds all the heavenly spheres
In their proper place.

Some say: you were born
At the same moment as the Big Bang,
And started flying forward as an arrow.
Others say: you're a product of our mind,
Going in circles of the same kind.

Mathematicians find you capable
Of flying in opposite directions
Without breaking down their equations
Or their models of the Universe.
So abstract is your supposed existence!

Now, O Time, please tell me:
Who are you exactly?
And, do you live in our minds
Or outside—as an independent entity
Luring us to become a part of singularity?

◌ 152 ◌
Man Will Rise Again
──────────────── ○ ────────────────

In my unbelief, I still believe:
Man is destined to rise again
From his lost place of esteem
Following his presumed fall
From Heaven's fitful grace
Because of Adam's mistake.
I can't believe God is so small
Or so vengeful—at all!

Though superior to angels,
Man isn't closer to his God
Whom he himself fashioned
And placed in his heart,
Reverently calling Him "Lord";
Presuming Him to be all-seeing
All-knowing, all-caring, and All;
Yet, Man's image remains small.

Though He gave us a short life span,
We must do all we can to rise again
In his due and proper esteem,
And regain the place we have lost.
This can't be done by begging
Or praying, or by just believing
That He is a placatable being
Who can be manipulated with ease,
Simply by falling on our knees.

Fully aware of Man's great efforts
And achievements here on earth
And there in space,—using his

Enlarged vision and technology
based on pure math and science—
Establishing many political, legal,
Social, ethical, and fiscal systems—
Yet, our God is not fully pleased!

Why, why, why? And why not?
Could it be that He values only
Our Obedience and Submission!
I don't believe He is so small,
Or unsure of his own greatness.
I believe He sees in us a colossal
Weakness: pride, apathy, sloth,
Greed, and self-centeredness.

Man must first believe in himself
That he can do whatever is needed
To alleviate his and others' pain
And suffering, and eliminate greed,
Ignorance, arrogance, anger and lies;
And all other tendencies that keep us
From being who we actually are
Supposed to be in our God's eyes.

So, we must first hone our conscience,
And shed our base tendencies that
Keep us from God's favor and esteem.
This will need a greater awareness
Of our Self and of cosmic consciousness,
For these two are supposed to go together.
Only then, the humankind will regain
Its lost position—and rise in Gods eyes.

൙ 153 ൫
Heart and Soul

─────────── o ───────────

We talk of soul,
Believing
It dwells in us,
Not knowing
Its real origin,
Nature, or goal.

We use our mind
To explore
This world and more,
Without finding
What connects it
To our soul.

Then we ask
Our heart quietly,
"What should we do
To connect the two?"
The heart replies,
"Fill me with love,
And
That will do."

℃ 154 ℬ
Waiting

My soul has wandered
Ahead of me
In search of him,
Whom I am dying to see.

My heart is throbbing
Fast enough to kill me,
Yet my eyes are still
Waiting for him patiently.

My sensate body of clay
Is slowly giving away
To thirst and exhaustion,
But I must find my own way.

Yes, I may lose my body
And mind imminently,
But my hope is locked
In my soul permanently.

❦ 155 ❧
Joe's Faith

———————————— ○ ————————————

The road is too dusty and long,
Winding uphill through knotted roots
Of the old gnarled trees that throng
The rocky steep—hard to walk on.

Traveler Joe is tired and weary
Of the overhead pulsating sun,
Making his eyes teary with sweat,
Yet his climb is only half done.

The trees are bare and sapless—
Their leaves snatched by searing wind.
The stunted shadows fanning helplessly
Provide no shade or heat rescind.

But weary Joe keeps trudging on,
Breathing through his clenched teeth,
Straining the sinews of a heavy heart.
And he knows not what is in his lot.

Though exhausted, his will is strong,
Upheld by his firm faith in the Lord
That he'll see his Nina ere too long,
Before her spirit is recalled by God.

He knew she wasn't feeling too well,
For she had sent him an urgent word
To see her, before she stumbled and fell
Under some spell he hadn't heard of.

He keeps on marching to beat the death,
Which he presumes is nearing the bed
Where she is holding to her last breath,
To tell him what had remained unsaid.

The sun is down; the twilight has set.
Poor Joe is now near the cottage door,
Glad that he may have finally won the bet.
But, alas, his dear love is there no more.

He drops to his knees by the bedside,
Lowers his face to kiss her closed eyes,
Pulls her cold hands gently to his side,
Trying to wake her to life with his cries.

But she is now dead to his and her lies,
Lies that had once sustained his belief
That their love would soar in the skies
As his shackles came off—to his relief.

About a year back, Joe had been charged,
With his friend, Jon, for selling a drug.
But Jon, the sole culprit, had enlarged
His net—and framed Joe with a shrug.

While Joe was sentenced to 180 days,
Jon was free to do as he darkly chose:
He set up another intrigue like a maze
With silky lies, as is done only by foes.

Slumped in grief by dead Nina's bed,
Joe lifts her hands to kiss and console,
But finds therein a note written in red
And reads it twice to sink it in—whole.

Nina's note was straight as an arrow:
"Joe, your absence drove me to Jon,
Who saved me from my loneliness,
But left me pregnant and in this mess."

Joe was crushed as never ever before.
His faith in friendship, love, and God
Was being tested; he felt, therefore,
Urged to pray for Nina to his dear Lord.

He stood up gracefully to his full height
Near the footboard of cold Nina's bed,
Lifted his strong hands above his head
And said, "God, give my love your light."

ᘓ 156 ᘒ
Healing

―――――――― ◊ ――――――――

The patient asked the healer, with a deep bow,
"What must be healed in sickness and how?"

"Body, mind, and soul," the healer replied.
"The body is the temple that nature supplied,
The mind its door, store, and reason's floor,
The soul its divine dweller, existent before."

The weary patient humbly ventured again,
"Body and mind with treatment may regain,
But why would soul, the indwelling divine,
Need healing? That I can't easily combine."

The sage replied, "Not for itself, but to regain
The lost connection between the three again;
So that the strings that play the melody best
Are in harmony and their discord put to rest."

At this the patient's eyes caught a bright gleam
From the light of wisdom—vital to redeem.

✂ 157 ✌
Truth Heals

——————— 0 ———————

There's little gain in hiding
What's clearly hanging out.
Bad faith can't be residing
In hearts that honesty spout.

When all is said and done,
There isn't much to guess,
Or look for a smoking gun
On a person ready to confess.

Truth and falsehood reside
Side by side in our minds,
Each side trying hard to undo
The other simply to hide

Our inherent imperfection,
Making us fear the truth
More often than our lies,
Thus enticing us to mislead.

So, telling the plain truth,
When mistrust has grown
In our close relationships,
There trust can be re-sown.

⚬₰ 158 ౖ

Pleasure and Pain
———————— o ————————

Pleasure and pain come and go.
The marks they leave are so
Wrought-up with our ego
And the perseverance we show.

Life's joys and sorrows bear
Witness to our growing, rearing
Fortitude, like a mother caring,
Rocking her child out of its fear.

The joy of genuine pleasures
May lift us to touch the stars;
The pain of sorrows measures
Our will to break down the bars.

Grief and sorrow remind us how
Blind creatures feed and survive
In the murkiest waters somehow,
And how, by mercy, Job did revive.

Life's pleasures we must embrace,
For these are gifts given in grace
By the Providence who sees it all—
Our willed actions great or small.

Pleasure and pain come and go;
Both are fleeting in their flow.
Embrace pleasure gratefully so;
Embrace pain without stooping low.

❧ 159 ☙
Choices

―――――――――――― ○ ――――――――――――

You like it hot
For you can trot
With whatever you got
After daringly sought
With no thought
As your lot

I like it cold
For I'm told
It is a way wiser to hold
Than to be easily sold
On fool's gold
So I fold

An idea or belief
Held in a sheaf
Of molded leaf over leaf
Gives the soul no relief
But only grief
And disbelief

A love too warm
Folded in charm
May send bells of alarm
Warning of some harm
Twisting the arm
Has no form

A promise made
May quickly fade
In hot sun, not so in shade

Drying it on the table laid
In sly charade
Shouldn't jade

What do we gain
Other than pain
By the hot desires that strain
Our heads and hearts disdain
And duly drain?
It is so plain.

❦ 160 ❧
Innocence

———— o ————

You say you have lost your innocence!
Is it your credence or flagrance speaking
Or for some reason your heart aching
Unspeakably, so pricking your conscience?

How is it possible! When the snow is white
Even in the dark night, and the dewdrops shine
Like dazzling diamonds in the first rays of light,
Waking you up, like an angel in delight.

Is innocence an ornament worn and unworn?
Or like a feature on the body that gets torn—
As in the case of virgins raped and forlorn,
Then on the forked tongues of gossip borne!

Innocence is the sweetest fragrance of the soul
That graces some, if not all, whatever be its dole.
But no one has ever disputed its noble role;
Innocence has not only one meaning or goal.

It's a virtue much praised and pleasant to behold.
It makes childhood winsome, curious, and bold.
It makes youth on beauty, love, and promise sold.
It makes the aged bear their heavy crosses untold.

Innocence in humankind seeks equality for all—
In their treatment, toil, recompense, and reward.
Innocence must not ever be silenced for a gain,
Nor must it, for any whim or necessity, be slain.

ॐ 161 ॐ
The Double

————— o —————

On an August afternoon,
With no reason to swoon,
As I was walking briskly down the lane
To meet a new lady friend from Tulane,
I figured my shadow was in some pain,
Trying to keep up in a reluctant strain.

For at every turn and bump in the lane
He visibly shrank or stretched or bent,
No matter how fast or slow I went;
He was plainly showing me his disdain.

My *own* shadow was acting most crazy,
Making me nervous ahead of my date
With this woman who was called Daisy;
And it was getting already far too late.

But I couldn't ignore my shadow's pain,
For it affected me too to no end or gain.
So I began to play the same trick again:
Cajoling him to calm down and remain

Vigilant to see the purpose of my quest
And not judge me by my nervous haste
Or whatever he thought a mere waste
Of time, but keep his patience at its best.

So I began to talk with him as earnestly
As I could about things not so mundane,
But which needed to come out honestly
To ease my raw conscience and his pain.

I asked my shadow, gently, "What ails thee?
Why do you shudder whenever I want to free
Myself of the fetters of fear that bind me?
My solitary existence I don't care to see."

On this, he lifted himself from the ground
And said, "You think your motives are sound,
But your choices have often had you so misled;
Your heart isn't in keeping with your head."

Just then, the sun went down,
And there rose the pale moon.

☙ 162 ❧
I Beseech You

— o —

Once again, I beseech you
Not to feel forlorn.
For a tree to be fruitful,
It can't bear when alone.

Good company is a boon
That doesn't dent solitude.
The bees visit a flowering tree
To bring it to fruit in plentitude.

This world, by its necessity,
Isn't alone or withdrawn
From other spheres of our galaxy,
But remains to them a paragon.

Don't be distraught, I implore,
By the attention you receive!
You will soon explore
The world, and duly perceive.

ॐ 163 ॐ
Power of Emotions

———————— o ————————

When emotions shape our thoughts,
Arising from our heads or hearts,
We simply assume our ideas are right;
This assumption bends our insight.

Emotions speak to us louder than logic,
Pulling us in with their power of magic,
As seen in conjugal love and religions:
Both invoking faith—with diligence.

But isn't faith based on an emotion
Inculcated with zeal and devotion?
Cleverly suggesting, "Not to question
But to believe and trust the equation;
Whether it is balanced square and fair,
For faith alone will all our doubts clear!"

So working on our emotions thus,
We readily believe without any fuss,
Those who for their benefit love us,
Including the cult or religion we profess.

In this way, our thought is shaped
And in a full suite of emotions draped;
Yet we boast of being very objective
While our thoughts are just subjective.

Though pure logic should be our guide,
And in reasoning we should take pride,
Humans more often emotions like,
For they easily show our love or dislike.

∞ 164 ∞
Drawing a Line

―――――――――― o ――――――――――

Where do you draw the line
When the issues of heart or head
Burn your blood fuming red?
Or stretch your nerves too fine!

We face this dilemma often
In our real or imagined lives,
Yet this canker bug thrives,
Turning our heads into beehives.

Then our conscience is tested
In the dim caves of thought,
As a fly in a spiderweb caught:
Trying to escape is quickly wasted.

But lines can easily be drawn
In our broad mental space,
Assigning each issue its own place,
Where novel ideas may spawn.

Segregated thus, they won't colloid
Or raise a din of cacophony
Or appear to be so deadly,
But certainly some solutions provide.

So where to draw a line?
No, not in the sand, air, or water
And not also in a state of anger,
But in *your* mind, where it will shine.

❦ 165 ❧
Second Chances

——————————— o ———————————

Sometimes happiness returns
Without any announcements,
Entering silently through a gate
That was once closed by ill fate.

The hurts and dejections we feel
(That make us close our hearts)
Do sometimes miraculously heal,
And then a new happiness starts.

When the dust of our dreams
A cruel wind has blown away,
New dreams take their place
And hold us in their own sway.

Then time seems to stand still,
Holding us in its balmy embrace,
Quickening our heart's pace,
Restoring our hopes with grace.

Happiness we must surely claim,
But our sorrows too have an aim;
For to sense the sweetness of joy,
We should know our pain's ploy.

This cyclical design is revealed
In the workings of the universe,
Which pulsates like a live being,
Preserving its functions diverse.

So when happiness knocks again,
Be willing to open all the doors
Of your heart's empty chamber,
To let her in with her healing force.

α 166 εο
Responsibility

─────────── o ───────────

You left it for me
To perceive and react
When I didn't see you
Unreasonably act.

I trusted you more
Than my own instinct,
For love was at its core,
So I never felt hoodwinked.

Now, if my blindness
Led you to squander
Your virtues to wickedness,
How can I your stains launder?

You are still perfect
In my blind eyes.
Now it's up to you to select
A way to reach the skies.

C� 167 �

Promenade

———————— o ————————

Two elegant rows of elm trees,
With sturdy trunks and green leaves
On all the extending branches borne,
A brick-lined promenade adorn.

Not narrow, curving, or short,
The promenade brings to life
The lovers walking abreast
In full display of their blissful art.

The lovers pause to admire
The two stands of rustling trees
That reach across and touch each other
Through the blue sky—and want to know

The truth that lies within all
And implores us to recall
What love needs most to be true and tall,
Besides an ardent heart to make its call.

The promenade through the trees
Provides a path to knowing this truth:
The leaves touching above tell us how to feel;
The light dancing below teaches us to kneel.

ଔ 168 ଈ
The Rain

————————————— o —————————————

The rain lost its angry bluster
Within an hour of beating hard
On the roses growing in a cluster
On a raised bed in my backyard.
The rain's fury didn't last long,
But its effect on me was strong.

The outburst of the untimely rain,
I felt, was not to my liking at all.
But when I saw the desolate plain,
Denuded, behind my garden wall,
It dawned on me that this storm
Would do more good than harm.

My neighbor's piece of dry land,
Where grasses struggle to grow,
Is just a wide bar of coarse sand
With not much to graze or mow
When clouds are dry or scarce,
And the sky sheds but few tears.

But when the rain blesses the land,
The emerald hidden in the sand
Comes alive as gay clover and grass
And gives the livestock a happy pass.
As this truth touched my heart,
I and my roses ceased to smart.

❧ 169 ❧
The Weeping Willow

The willow was weeping, yet
Keeping her green eyes fixed
On the rivulet running below,
Dreading when its rapid flow
Might slow down, then cease
Altogether; for the crops above
Need their lifeblood to keep
The farmers in their business.

There were other reasons too
For the willow's deep sorrow:
Her friend, the rainbow trout,
Would leave her for a stream
Running full to please its gills.
The doves too wouldn't come
To sit and sing on her boughs,
Pouring songs from their bills.

The willow's fears grew anew
Each day; the breath she drew
Became a dry, murmuring sigh,
Beseeching Zephyr for his aid
To make the hot summer fade
With cool air and cloudy shade
And some rain to ease her pain.
Soon God answered her prayer.

৫৪ 170 ৡৡ
Our Hope

— o —

When we cry
In the wilderness,
Bitten by our loneliness,
Do You hear us?

Yes, yes, surely—
We presume we are blessed;
If we didn't believe so certainly,
How else would we be solaced!

Yet our fears,
Lurking behind our hopes,
Drown us in blinding tears,
Pushing us down the slippery slopes.

But we are sustained
By Your love and mercy.
This hope is firmly retained
In our breast as a prophecy.

ᘓ 171 ᘒ
What Is Better?
—————————— o ——————————

Is it better to be a fool or a clever person?
Let's figure it out, dear son, and be done.

******

The fool knows little, but has some fun
Basking on a beach, loving earth and sun,
Sleeping under the stars, worrying none.

The clever one has no time for such kicks,
For he is too busy sharpening his tricks
To run down others with his gleeful smirks.

A real fool is eager to please everyone,
Ready to put all his belongings on lease
To pay for his friends' delinquent fees.

The clever one uses charm to inflict harm
In ways too cunning to raise any alarm
And by fake pleasantry to win and disarm.

The fool employs simpler ways to please:
His comic ignorance, innocence, and ease,
Which endear him to others in a breeze.

A clever guy uses others as a perfect tool
To advance his own mischievous plans,
Then subjects the helping hand to ridicule.

So, while the fool plays from spring to fall,
The clever make life a harsh winter for all.
Now, my son, who would you prefer to be?
Look at this paradox closely, and decide freely.

❦ 172 ❧
Be a Victor

---○---

Let us move forward
Without a backward look;
Mistakes made in the past
Must not hook or bind us
In the Gordian knots
That can't be untied,
Except by a novel thought,
As the great Alexander applied.

So let's move ahead and join
The victors who don't get bogged
In the swampy theaters
Where old alligators of fear and doubt
Prevail, propagate, and regale,
Eating us from inside out.

Victors and victories
Fill the pages of history,
With wars fought to free or enslave;
But there are other battles too
That we fight every day,
Challenging our valor in another way.

These battles are fought in our hearts,
Where prowess alone is not enough;
But mastering the self is required,
For selflessness is the victor's ground,
And love and care his throne.

ᙕ 173 ᙖ
Selflessness

———————— 0 ————————

Yes, to be immune
To loss or gain,
Pleasure or pain,
Is seen by saints and sages
As an uplifting virtue
That shields us from sorrow.

Some construe this to mean
That we shouldn't on feelings lean
Or possess any sensitivity,
For these traits make us weak;
So let us be rather insensitive,
And indifference seek!

But a lack of feelings
For others' grim suffering,
Destitution, or disease
Also lends to more suffering
That noble hearts dread
Seeing or imposing.

For it destroys
Our faith in humanity,
And sorrows find no relief
As the unfeeling keep on
Selling with impunity
Their conscience to Grief.

These contrary views
Beg to be settled thus:
If moved by your gain or loss,
You are weak and selfish;
If moved by others' heavy cross,
You are strong and selfless.

∽ 174 ∾
Faith

—o—

Too long to bondage Reason was consigned,
Chained by Religion, tyrant of the mind.
—Lucretius, *On the Nature of Things*

—o—

Some say they have seen the truth eternal,
Hidden in their hearts and vaguely supernal,
Through a reflection of the word paternal
That rapidly evolved into a faith fraternal.

Driven by a passion to remain united in a fold,
No one dares to question and break the hold
Of ideas that are hackneyed and definitely old,
Yet powerful enough to render judgment cold.

Each group and sect in its truth finds some rest
And considers it as the ultimate and the best;
In this conceit, they plunder, pillage, and test
The faith of another and stomp it into dust.

The civilized factions use a gentler approach:
They proselytize, preach, teach, and coach
To give up your belief and adopt their faith,
Promising everlasting love, life, and the wraith.

Like the frogs in a narrow well, they can't see
That there are waters much larger than a cup of tea,
Some deep 'n' clear, some rich in pearl as in the sea;
But, alas, all they can see is my, mine, and me!

◌ 175 ◌
Split Images
─────────○─────────

Shards of a broken mirror
Speak with many faces,
Each exhibiting its terror
Of the split self it encases.

Similar is the fate of love
That can't keep its breath
In reaching the stars above,
And thus crashes to its death.

Pieces of a picture puzzle,
When put together alright,
May delight and dazzle us,
Yet their outlines do affright.

Stray remarks rearranged
Can be taken differently:
Bleakly by the estranged,
Rightly by the unchanged.

ॐ 176 ॐ
The Truth

———— o ————

Truth is a goddess:
beautiful and sublime,
of many forms and functions,
existential and transcendental,
showing what is real and ethical:
veracity, faithfulness, and fidelity.

Truth can be too bitter or sweet;
she can lift you off your feet
or throw you on your face,
but in either case
she will make you wiser,
even richer, never a miser.

Truth may reveal her face
by God's grace,
but she is too difficult to find,
for she is not so kind
to each and every one,
seeking her with reverence none.

Truth lies hidden
in the caverns of mystery,
mind, matter, and shards of history,
awaiting love and labor to yield
the facts necessary to reveal
her true identity concealed.

Truth may want us to stay afloat
like a lotus on serene waters, and wait,
or plunge in a Promethean urge

to meet her at the subterranean gate,
just for a little wisdom to gain
that would lessen our existential pain.

Truth may sometimes clash
with her child called Civility,
causing hurt feelings—even animosity;
but one can't gag the truth
or exchange her for untruth,
as civility can't hide truth's luminosity.

We often refrain
from scratching the surface,
for fear of knowing the truth
about our beliefs, desires, and actions,
others' feelings, responses, and reactions,
and thus prefer to remain uncouth.

ॐ 177 ॐ
What I Want

—————————— 0 ——————————

I know what I want now and why,
On this earth and beyond the sky,
Conscious or unconscious I may lie
While alive, and even after I die.

Power, glory, or fame I don't need.
Riches or rewards aren't my mead.
On pure knowledge I want to feed.
From ego's hold I want to be freed.

Add one more thing to these gifts,
Dear God, give me love that uplifts,
Saving us from falling into icy drifts
Of wily indifference and deep rifts.

Fill me with sweet breath of love,
That I may on its wings soar above
The abyss of hate—a thirsting dove
Searching for You bough to bough.

I see You in every branch and leaf.
I see: You are central to each belief.
Every being and soul seeks relief.
So do I—from my existential grief.

So I beg for that kind of wisdom—
Suffused with love—seen seldom,
Which is needed for a soul's freedom
To secure a place in Your kingdom.

Ꮭ 178 ᏚᏅ
Whence I Come

———————— o ————————

I didn't come here on my own.
(It wasn't in my power to do so.)
You cast me from Yourself—as a stone
Thrown in a live dimension of space,
Requiring me now to find my place
With my free will to figure and find:
Whence I come, where must I go?

You are the king sitting on the hill;
I am the arrow shot from your bow.
It all started from Your own will,
So how come I am responsible
To find my way in a valley so low?
All I know is what I sense and feel:
Whence I come, there I want to go.

I know you like to dance and play,
To revel in your own manifestation;
And it pleases you to mold the clay
Around a soul to seek its destination,
Knowing well its natural inclination
To reach its home (You) with no delay;
Whence I come, there I must go.

So why have you sent me here
To struggle through a jungle of pain—
Sufferings of love and hate to endure?
What joy or knowledge is there to gain
In descending from mountain to plain?
Am I right? Or do I err or perjure?
Whence I come, there I shall go.

❧ 179 ❧
Belonging

———————— o ————————

For a long time I believed
The things I had acquired
With effort or ease—
For me to advance or shine
Or my ego to please—
Were really mine.

Then one day I woke up
From my deep sleep
In a new world of sunshine,
Where I could easily leap
And grasp the cup
I drink from, which is Thine.

Things I thought were mine—
My life, loves, and yearnings,
My career and earnings,
Things needed or unneeded,
Received often unimpeded—
Are actually Thine.

At times I asked for more,
As my desires kept a score.
You gave me what I needed;
Thy warning I never heeded.
Though it rang clear as a bell,
I couldn't its meaning tell.

Then it slowly came to me—
Not from any loss or sorrow,
But from a vision very fine—
That I am eternally Thine,

With all my belongings
—life, learning, and longings—
So grant me Thy love to acquire.
That's the only thing I require.

ॐ 180 ॐ
My Divine Friend

——————————————— o ———————————————

No measure of being can measure You.
No height is sufficient to reach You.
No depth is deep enough to fathom You.
No shape or form is perfect to match You.

I sense your presence always around me.
I sense your presence always within me.
But, alas! I can't see you with my eyes,
Nor, alas, can I reach you with my cries.

Why do you play these tricks with me?
Why do you first engage with me?
Why do you then disengage with me?
Why do you play hide-and-seek with me?

Is it because we are so different?
Is it because you are so indifferent?
Is it because you are too distant?
Or is it because we are one?

If you love me, indeed, as they say,
If you made me in your image, as they say,
If you want my adoration, as you command,
Help me know You better, I humbly demand.

ೞ 181 ഔ
You and Me

I am a vessel
Made of clay.
You fill me again and again
With your breath—to play.

In this way,
We have become one.
Like the tide and ocean,
Our union can't be undone.

Your presence,
Both far and near,
Ensures my existence,
Without any doubt or fear.

But for You I couldn't be;
Without creating me,
You wouldn't be happy.

↶ 182 ↷
The Two Paths
———————— o ————————

You have chosen
The path of love and devotion
—Bakhti-Yoga[1]—
For your liberation,[2]
Flying on the wings of a dove
Far above the path of knowledge
—Janana-Yoga[3]—
Avoiding the serpent and the tree.

You follow the words
Of Krishna and Christ:
The promised life through love,
A simple path ensuring your tryst
With the personal God
Who redeems His devotee
By returning his love,
With grace, accordingly.

I try to seek Him
In His imminent form
Revealed before our eyes
In all the seasons, sounds, and seas,
In the leaves of grass and the galaxies.
For the path of knowledge (Janana)
Unites one with the Holy Spirit
Of Brahman[4], eternally.

---

1 Path of love
2 Salvation, Moksha, Nirvana
3 Path of knowledge
4 Godhead: absolute truth, pure consciousness, and complete bliss.

Yes, spiritual knowledge
May lead us to the Transcendent,
But it is not possible for all.
The very few who try and succeed

Have truth and grace on their side
And find a place in the self of God.
But for those like you and me,
Let love our path to Him be.

You have accepted the world
As it is, by seeing and sorting
And by lovingly consorting
With samsara's[1] ebb and flow;
You freed your mind of its doubt
By choosing love over knowledge.
You are content with what you know,
But I have yet in this respect to grow.

---

1 The ever-changing world/universe

❧ 183 ☙
Longing

—— o ——

I keep rushing
Down the mountain
Like a thirsty stream
In search of the ocean
To quench my thirst
For perpetual motion.

I keep blowing
Through groves of trees
Like a fierce, whipping wind,
Searching for the fallen leaves
Of the tree of knowledge
That, for no reason, grieves.

I keep dashing
Like a hungry lion
To catch the fleeting prey,
But with no appetite today,
I let it run away,
For my mane has turned gray.

Now I ask God
For my deliverance
From this commotion
That keeps me on the run,
Serving no purpose or fun
Except pumping my emotion.

໙ 184 ໖
Light Supreme

---- ◊ ----

Hail holy Light, offspring of Heav'n first born,
Or of the Eternal coeternal beam
May I express the unblamed? Since God is light.
—John Milton, *Paradise Lost, Book 3*

---- ◊ ----

Oh! what can I do without You,
    Who has hidden His countenance
Behind the sun and stars—not few
    But all—imitating Your brilliance,

Making it difficult to understand
    Who is who, and who the shaker
Of light in this universe grand?
    Who the mover? Who the maker?

If it's true You are the source of light,
    Then why are there so many stars
Bent on hiding You from my sight?
    Could it be they are Your avatars?

If I knew, I would fly to You faster
    Than light, on the wings of thought
(Painted in gold on white alabaster),
    Fueled by poesy in my craving heart.

As I am waiting for this truth to dawn,
    I breathe, eat, sleep, dream, and rise—
Just to be alive—but remain withdrawn,
    Until I see You with my own eyes.

Dear God, illuminate me with a vision
        Of Your real form and presence;
It would dispel my darkest confusion.
        I can't do it without your guidance.

ༀ 185 ༀ
Grace and Karma

—————————— o ——————————

Man is lost without God's grace.
Love's loss nothing can replace.
Wealth and power have a place,
But loss of either is no disgrace.

Grace is a gift of divine mercy,
Shown to those who err but remain
In God's far reaching eye still worthy.
The rest of us are bound to causality.

Cause and effect are linked eternally;
The law of karma governs inherently.
When deception is practiced indulgently,
Misfortune attends to it imminently.

The goodness you show never forego.
To bad feelings and actions say no.
The fair and foul times come and go;
They are just transitory in their flow.

Wait for your action's fruit to ripen,
For it will in its sweet time happen.
With learning let your mind sharpen;
With love in your heart, it'll brighten.

The air in a vessel may give us a sign
Of its separate existence from Thine,
You are in all, yet we bow in a shrine;
This illusion of duality we deem fine.

God is not a subject among subjects.
God is not an object among objects.
The whole universe resides in Brahman[1].
As it manifests, a man-god resurrects,
But in truth, only Brahman exists.

---

1 Supracosmic godhead, the imminent and transcendental principle of existence; absolute truth, pure consciousness, and complete bliss.

෴ 186 ෴
Star of Bethlehem

—————————— o ——————————

O Star of Bethlehem, lead me there,
Where a baby's breath filled the air,
Spreading light in the darkened cave
Of human mind—in order to save it.

Here God was born to toil and try
As a man, and to plant the seeds of love
In the arid lands and hearts that cry
Out for rain to wet them somehow.

My heart and mind are thirsting too
For the blest shower of such a rain
That makes the seeds of love to move
And grow into flowers without strain.

The son of man, who was born to die
And to rise again, fills me with awe;
I beg him to reside in my mind's eye,
For in him the miracle of God I saw.

Walking the talk under the blazing sun,
He showed how to be strong and kind
And to forgive those who have us undone;
For it's a sure way we can happiness find.

O Star of Bethlehem, lead me there:
Where truth and vision are quite clear,
Where the light of love shines on our path,
Purging our souls from greed and wrath.

ఆ 187 శీ
Thank You

———————— o ————————

Thank you, dear God, for making me be
Of humankind, to see this world and find
Thy divine Lila[1] in space, time, and mind—
All, in adoration, to see, contained in Thee.

Though my time is short and brief,
This gives me no trouble, doubt, or grief;
Each moment of my life is richly filled,
As Thy love and grace keep me thrilled.

So why should I fear that my time is near?
I know deep in my soul You are there
To show me the way—then take me away,
As I awaken to your Maya's[2] incredible sway.

In animating this lump of Prakritic[3] clay,
Thy spark changed me from night into day;
There is nothing I want to have or save.
Oh God, I am thankful for the gift You gave.

Your precious gift of life enjoins us to see
The parts and purpose of all there can be,
From the tiny atom to the largest galaxy,
Primitive impulse to science and technology.

———————————————————

1 Divine play/activity; divine dispensation
2 Power by which the phenomenal world is created/manifested
3 Material cause of nature/world—in Sankhya philosophy

My deliverance, Moksha,[1] will not easily come
Until my soul has completely Yours become.
Oh, could love and knowledge take me there!
But first: grace and devotion are needed here.

---

1   Attainment of liberation / salvation / nirvana

ભ 188 ഓ
At the End of the Day

———————————— o ————————————

Oh! the day has ended
Sooner than I expected;
Now how can I complete
All the neglected tasks
That scream "Incomplete."

The time to go has come.
I'll shed my clothes now,
Lighten my load somehow,
For I've to go on a journey.
Let my tasks incomplete be.

I can't keep Him waiting,
For there is a price to pay,
Far greater than to meet
The unmet obligations that lay
Golden traps under my feet.

He knows why I failed
To carry my cross to Calvary.
He knows how I was assailed
By doubt and attendant strife;
But I have His word of afterlife.

ೞ 189 ೲ
Being and Becoming
———————— o ————————

These countless spheres
Hanging out in space—
Some young, some old,
Some hot, some cold;
One of them a live planet blue,
Others give us no plausible clue.
But what purpose to their maker—
God or nature—do they serve?

Likewise, countless forms
Of life on this planet Earth,
Simple to most complex,
Their cells or muscles flex
And show cognitive intelligence
Ascending from molecule to man.
But I wonder why their maker—
God or nature—made it so happen?

Most believe God made the universe
For He felt lonely and lovelorn;
Others say it was nature's doing,
For natural laws keep on going.
These notions invoke some emotion
But fail to satisfy a simple question:
How can a self-sufficient God be lovelorn?
How would nature by itself be born?

This riddle is not easy to solve,
Unless all parties resolve
To bring a light of thought without blame
And see: the maker and the things made

May be one and the same;
For God may have created the universe
To discover and enjoy His own being,
Becoming many out of one Truth or Law.

☙ 190 ❧
Brahman

———————— o ————————

My being was before my becoming.
In thee, O Brahman,[1] all was dwelling,
Unmanifest, nirguna,[2] formless,
Undifferentiated, in pure consciousness.
In truth and bliss existence was reveling.

Then love arose in cosmic splendor.
Self separated from the Supreme Self
As light from thunder;
Spirit entered the primordial matter
To enjoy Thy manifestation in wonder.

Nirguna became Saguna,[3] the Isvara.[4]
Matter gave means of sense perception,
Ego and individuation without exception.
But my spirit was now caught in a vase;
Thus bound and limited, I lost my place.

My fall from heaven made me wander
From form to form, here and yonder,
To find my way home;
In cycles of birth and death I emerge
Again and again, only to submerge.

——————————

1 Supracosmic Godhead
2 Brahman without attributes
3 Brahman with attributes—personal God, Ishvara
4 God the Creator

Submerge in the infinite ocean of bliss,
Eternal truth and pure consciousness—
Liberation, Moksha[1], Nirvana.
The homeward journey must now start;
My being must submerge in "Thou Art."

---

1 Liberation from cycles of birth and death (Atman's merger with Brahman)

ଓ 191 ଓ

Atman[1]

———————— o ————————

I am the light of the sun and the stars
That illumines my way on this planet,
And through the sky into deep space
As I journey to my inner resting place.

I am the earth, the air, and the fire,
All the plants that drape this sphere,
All creatures of land, water, and air,
Respiring to keep the fire of life near.

I am the river, its ripples and flow,
Swelling the ocean—which too I am—
And the laden cloud of blessings grand
Falling as rain on the seas and land.

I am the moving dot of consciousness,
Expanding—so creating the universe,
With all its raw matter and motion,
Like a wave riding an infinite ocean.

I am the song, the singer, and the listener,
The melody flowing forth as Kala, the time.
I am the voice of silence, as one can tell;
I am closer to you than heaven or hell.

---

1 Soul, the deepest self of man; a spark of Brahman;
some equate Atman with Brahman

I am the truth of each subject and object.
I am the mind and the intellect that guide
One through the darkest period of night
To find true knowledge, bliss, and light.

৩ 192 ৯

The Sense of I

———————————— o ————————————

With the sense of I, I have become one
With the earth, the moon, and the sun,
And see the whole Universe within me
As my consciousness expands steadily.

Though a life-form in this world, I am
In each particle of matter and energy,
Dancing as the Purusha[1] and the Prakrati[2]
In the iconic forms of Shiva[3] and Parvati.[4]

My kinship with my brother and sister,
My love for you, O miss and mister,
Is simply tied to this divine necessity:
That we are One despite our diversity.

---

1 Informing and sustaining soul (in Sankhya philosophy)
2 Matter or material basis of an individual/world/universe
3 One of three faces (divine aspects) of Hindu trinity constituting Ishvara (God)
4 Shiva's consort (shakti or power)—envisioned as the female principle

ೞ 193 ೮೨
The Tavern
—————————————— o ——————————————

This old tavern is teeming
  With many a thirsty soul,
Each one of them seeming
  To pursue a different goal.

They've come here empty-eyed
  To catch a glimpse of truth,
Hoping if they sincerely tried
  They may not remain uncouth.

So they look around avidly
  For some kindred spirit to find,
With whom they would sit quietly
  Emptying their burdened mind.

They guzzle many a bottle of wine—
  Some tinctured sweet, some dry,
Forgetting for what they so pine—
  No matter how hard they try.

All of them seem to agree
  That they are thirsty for love,
But, for whom and to what degree
  They must turn their eyes now.

Most of them are tethered to earth—
  Wanting to enjoy her delicious fruit;
A few disavow the Dionysian mirth,
  But crave for the Apollonian truth.

Neither is superior or inferior to other,
     As both paths lead to the same place;
All we have to do is: gather our senses
     And ignorance replace.

As sentient beings, we aren't alone
     Carrying a heavy cross of our being.
Look around without feeling forlorn—
     Our loneliness ends only on seeing:

That individual and cosmic Consciousness
Connect us All—here and beyond,
Despite any *difference* or *indifference*
We sense, see, or show.

෪ 194 ฌ
Amber Wine

——————————— o ———————————

Intoxicated by the Wine of Love
From each a mystic silence Love demands.
—Attar, *Jawhar Al-Dhat* (translated by Margaret Smith)

——————————— o ———————————

Amber! Amber!
My dear Amber,
Do you remember
When we met for the first time?
And thence walked together in rhyme,
As the seasons merrily marched by.

You were in a vintage store
Offering samples of wine indoor;
I too slowly sipped a few,
while conversing with you.
A warm wave traversed through me;
Its visible effect you could clearly see…

Then you took an ancient holy book
Out of your satchel—for me to take a look.
Recognizing it, I looked at you—totally amazed,
Then, inwardly, your wine and wisdom praised.
I could now easily figure out your true vocation:
You are a mystic yogi—given to deep meditation.

Your love of learning,
And the ways of seeking
The real meaning of Karma-Yoga—
That keep your lights burning—
Is a virtue I couldn't easily reach.
So, I begged you to be my guru, and teach.

৫ 195 ৯

Chetana[1]

—————————————— o ——————————————

O Chetana, wake me up
With your clarion call
When you see me develop
A tendency to flounder and fall.

And if I lose my consciousness
Catch me then in your arms
With the natural kindness
Which you show in multiple forms.

My mind is still in its game—
Sensing an urge in my Atman
To honestly admit and proclaim
That I need more of Chetana.

You always wake us up
With a gentle warning—whenever
You see us harming our own self
Or those around us—that we must
Hear and heed. So keep me awake
Under your ever-watchful eye.

---

1 Consciousness

❧ 196 ❧
Laurel Groves

―――――――――― ο ――――――――――

A Hyphen must connect Matter and Mind,
The narrow isthmus of the ascending soul.
—Aurobindo Ghose, *Savitri*, Book I, Canto IV

―――――――――― ο ――――――――――

Through the groves of laurel trees
I roam, asking myself how to claim
The only joy I feel impelled to seize—
Not the kind sought in a Pythian[1] game
Honored by a crown of laurel leaves.

I seek a prize of a different kind:
One that would open my inner eyes
To the mystery of Consciousness—
How does it arise? Where is it assigned?
In the brain, mind, or the universe!
And how can this knowledge be gained?

In these sacred groves, one can hear
The lingering echoes of a higher Vidya,[2]
That was revealed to the ancient seers
By the power of meditation and yoga:[3]
They gave this knowledge to their disciples
In the academies that stood in these groves.

They said: "Consciousness is the 'soul'[4] of Cosmos.
Every particle and being has it in varying degrees
Depending on the stage of their evolution

―――――――――――――

1 Greek games
2 Higher Knowledge
3 Union
4 Primary reality

And the extent of *information*[1] they contain.
Humans are by far self-aware,
But of deeper consciousness mostly unaware.

"As you shut your senses in deep meditation,[2]
You'll see a different world in you awaken:
Your Atman (soul), the real You in you,
And its connection with Brahman[3]
Progressively revealed to you."
It is this ancient knowledge
Of *Truth and Bliss* I was seeking
In the groves of laurel trees.

---

1   As in Information Theory
2   In Sanskrit: Smadhi
3   Cosmic Soul

ೞ 197 ೞ
The Yogi Says

———————————— o ————————————

The Yogi says:

Every day! I will take you away
Into the realm of consciousness
Where you will see your real Self
As *One* with *All* in the Universe,
Residing in eternal *Truth and Bliss*.
And you will then understand this:

> Life is for loving
> Life is for learning
> Life is for achieving
> Life is for daring
> Life is for sharing
> Giving and receiving—
> Joy to each other.

When your identity becomes cosmic
You are rid of: All tensions domestic
All delusions embedded in untruth
All fears fogging your will and resolve
All doubts holding you back from action
And you'll sense a limitless energy rising.

I ask the yogi:

> So, my dearest yogi,
> Teach me now: how
> Can I rightly embrace
> The whole Universe

When I see only you
In my consciousness—
Reveal this to me.

The yogi replies:

When we meditate to seek cosmic consciousness
We are rid of our narrow identity, for we are now
No longer under a small cone of light—as its angle
And circle widen to subtend all. The defining and
Confining boundaries of our bodies and personalities
Fade away, and our inner *Self, the real being,* is revealed.

As this light intensifies, we see the connection that
Our *being* and *consciousness* has with the Universe.
See: We inhale, absorbs and assimilate the same
Particles, waves, energy, and information that also
enter and belong to other living beings and Nature
– for making our bodies, brains, and the rest.

So, by sharing and interacting we become a part
of *Cosmic Consciousness* pervading the Universe—
Call this all—God or Existence.
This yoga (*union*) frees us.

๏ 198 ๏
Who Am I?

———————————— o ————————————

I am swallowed in a foam-white sea of bliss,
I am a curving wave of God's delight,"
—Aurobindo Ghose, "The Bliss of Brahman"

———————————— o ————————————

I am not I because *I think*,[1]
But I *think* because *I Am*:

Conscious of being alive—
While awake, dreaming, or in deep sleep.
My *being* (*self, atman*) is awash and awake
In the ocean of *Consciousness*, which is
The fundamental and primary reality
Of this universe of *Being* and *Becoming,*
Named by ancient rishis as *Brahman.*

If I were to choose
One thing above all,
I would a discerning eye
That sees clearly the truth in this:
Atman and *Brahman* are One—
Meaning: I live in God
And His *Light of Being* is in me.

———————————————

1 Descartes said, "Ergo cogito sum" meaning, "I think therefore I am." This view is being challenged here.

Thus, it is not *thinking*
That makes me self-aware
But the *consciousness* in me
Of my own existence
That empowers me to think,
Act and see.

ॐ 199 ॐ
The Blissful Consciousness

———————————— o ————————————

The flame of consciousness that burns bright
in my heart is not a fortuitous prisoner within
the narrow confines of life. That flame, which
at the beginning rises from the Void...
This Consciousness throbs through the skies
—Rabindranath Tagore, On the Sick-Bed

———————————— o ————————————

When you come—just to see me!
I sense your presence by the fragrance
That spreads around my comatose body, quickly
Dissipating the heavy air settled in the room,
Where I lie on the hospital bed—motionlessly.
Then my inner eyes open slowly...
And I begin to see:
    Seabirds over the waves their flights resume,
    Daffodils in my heart pumping heavenly perfume,
    Butterflies in my stomach its sweetness consume,
    The dead I once adored, their full statures assume,
While the doctors around me: Me dead presume!

When you sit—just next to me!
Holding my cold hand in your warm ones,
A burst of light from a thousand suns
Flashes through my injured brain suddenly,
Filling each of my neurons with divine energy,
Then my Atman enters into Brahman's reality...
And I begin to see:
    My soul merging with the Consciousness of Space,
    Dissolving into particles that barely leave a trace,

Smaller than the smallest with a distinct face,
Stretched out in the expanding cosmos as divine lace,
While the living think: I am only in one place!

Oh No! That isn't so; we all assemble and disassemble:
At times the particles aggregate into a conscious being
At times they are millions of light-years apart but entangled—
Talking to each other in fields and waves that may resemble
Those that arose when the primordial atom broke into Sound
In the *Ocean of Consciousness*, to *Truth and Bliss* bound.

❧ 200 ❧
My Prayer

───────── ○ ─────────

I rarely go to a temple, church, or a shrine,
But I love Thee dearly, and also pine.
So please tell me:
When and where shall I offer
My prayers to Thee,
O God Supreme?

At dawn!

When the sun and the birds
Are already up,
In joyous communion with Thee,
Offering wreathes of light and melody,
Reminding me
Of my insufficiency in words and voice
To praise Thee!

At dusk!

When thoughtful men and women,
With their uplifted eye,
Pray for you to appear in the starry sky,
The evening air and love that for You sigh;
My vision gets blurred
By tears of joy,
Choking my voice and word.

Day and night!

Dear God, I have heard
You are merciful and kind
To all—in keeping with Your word—
Even to those who are dumb and blind.
So, accept my prayers I silently make
Everywhere, all the time.

Index

Y

About the Book

The Beauty of Being Human by Dr. Nirander Safaya

In this collection of two hundred poems, written after retirement from a brilliant scientific career, author Nirander Safaya takes us on a panoramic journey of self-discovery. Collectively, these poems focus on: What it means to be human. Attachment to life, desire to love and be loved, curiosity and thirst for knowing, and self-awareness are the hallmarks of human nature. Dr. Safaya's poetry portrays the beauty and the challenges of these human gifts and aspirations.

The Beauty of Being Human shows how our lives can become truly beautiful and fulfilled by a conscious understanding of the gifts we sapiens possess. The book is thematically divided into three parts: part 1 has seventy poems on "Life and Living," part 2 has sixty-eight poems on "Love and Passion," and part 3 has sixty-two poems on "Light and Consciousness." By presenting the poems in a sequential order, the poet is taking the serious reader through a gradual unfolding of his aesthetic and philosophical vision of the pragmatic, romantic, and spiritual aspirations of the human heart and soul. It also provides a casual poetry lover the freedom to read these poems randomly and enjoy their message and beauty.

"Dazzling" and uplifting, the poetry of Nirander Safaya provides "surprising imagery… to uncommon and timeless effect." The joys and sorrows of life and the saving grace of light and consciousness are the topics and the "sensory delight" of this book.

About the Author

Dr. Nirander Safaya

Dr. Nirander Safaya taught and conducted research in physiology at various universities in India and the United States. He then served as the environmental sciences administrator for land reclamation in North Dakota until his retirement. He has authored many scientific papers and book chapters, and he has received awards for professional excellence. His first poetry book, ***Reflections on Being Human***, was published in 2016.

www.ingramcontent.com/pod-product-compliance
Lightning Source LLC
Chambersburg PA
CBHW070904120626
46546CB00001B/132